Filo!

Appetizers, Entrées & Desserts

by Jan Nix

The Crossing Press • Freedom, California 95019

I would like to thank Marguerite Dalienes, Michele Dumesnil, Mary Dalienes Mitchel, Lou Pappas, Anna Roder, and Esther Walkenshaw for treasures from their recipe files; Migirdich Sagatelyan and his brother Mihran of Sheherazade Bakery, who generously shared their knowledge in the art of commercial filo making; and Abby Nash, who first suggested the idea for this book and backed it up with three stellar recipes. My special thanks go to Linda Ziedrich for carefully editing the manuscript; Meg O'Malley who happily shared her creative energy; Margie Witt, who joined me in many pleasurable hours of testing and filo folding, and to my family and friends who have lent support and enthusiastic response to the making of this book.

Cover illustration and design by Ann Marie Arnold
Interior illustrations by Ann Marie Arnold
Printed in the U.S.A.

Library of Congress Cataloging-in-Publication Data

Nix, Janet Johnson.
    Filo! : appetizers, entrées & desserts / by Jan Nix.
           p. cm.
    Includes index.
    ISBN 0-89594-516-9 (cloth) -- ISBN 0-89594-515-0 (paper)
    1. Cookery (Filo dough)   I. Title.
TX770.F55N58 1991   91-24271
641.8--dc20   CIP

Contents

1
About Filo

For all the simplicity of its components—flour, water, and salt—tissue-thin filo (pronounced FEE-low) is a terrifically versatile dough in which hundreds of fillings can be wrapped to make mouth-watering appetizers, snacks, entrées, and sweets.

Filo originally earned its reputation in *baklava*, strudel, and Middle Eastern savories. Today, cooks who are looking for ways to trim minutes from busy schedules and trim calories from classic dishes are turning to filo as an easy, lightweight alternative to puff pastry and pie dough and as a stand-in for dough wrappers that must be deep-fried. Filo needs only an oven's dry heat to become crisp and flaky.

It's fun to work with filo. You can fold it, roll it, twist it, crinkle it, crumple it, and layer it to make spectacular-looking food, or you can simply stack it and turn it into a dramatic container to hold anything you want. Just as colorful paper and ribbon transform a simple gift into a delight, filo adds exciting visual quality to food and gives it great style.

While playful, filo is not frivolous. There is no better or easier coverup for leftovers. Generations of thrifty cooks have given new life to yesterday's dinner by recombining elements and wrapping them in filo. Professional cooks avert back-of-the-house disasters with filo fancies. But for most cooks, filo's strongest selling point is its make-ahead quality. With few exceptions, food can be wrapped in filo and chilled or frozen until ready to use for a simple family meal or grand-scale entertaining.

There's no mystery when you work with filo. It's a matter of chemistry. The sheets of dough are brushed with butter or oil, stacked in layers, and wrapped around a filling. Filo protects the filling so it stays moist, or, if the filling is runny, filo provides necessary structure. When a filo creation is baked, steam trapped inside puffs up the wrapper, and the filo browns and becomes the flaky buttery cover that crinkles in your mouth.

Despite opinions to the contrary, filo is easy to work with, but you must protect it from air. The parchment-thin sheets dry out quickly, so it is essential to keep those you are not at present folding covered at all times. Follow the keep-covered rule, and you'll find folding filo as simple as folding a sheet of tissue paper.

Commercial Filo Making

Although filo is easy to use, I do not suggest that you make the dough yourself. A look into the commercial filo making process and the filo making tradition will tell you why.

Before the advent of modern technology, filo dough was made by hand and sold to a local clientele. A filo maker could stretch 10 pounds of dough in 1 hour—a time consuming project even in the hands of a skilled worker. As the demand for filo and filo based products increased, the need arose to develop a machine that would automatically mass produce filo. Today most filo is made by a fully automated process. Machine made filo is widely distributed, fresh or frozen, throughout North America.

In some areas, it is still possible to find commercial filo made by hand. You may find a source listed in your telephone directory. But whether you use commercially rolled or hand stretched filo, the secret is to keep it covered to prevent drying out.

The Filo-Making Tradition

On December 31, 1990, Migirdich Sagatelyan closed the door of the Sheherazade Bakery in San Francisco. After 58 years of making filo, Middle Eastern pastries, and candy, crafts he learned from his father, he planned to retire.

I was fortunate to watch the filo making process on this last day of business. Let me paint you a picture. Mike, as he known to his friends, and his brother Mihran, who has 48 years of experience making filo, mixed high-gluten flour, water, and salt to form a dough that was divided into balls, covered with a damp towel, and left to rest for an hour. They then rolled each ball into a flat disk about 18 inches in diameter, sprinkled each with cornstarch, and stacked the disks one on top of the other.

Now it was time for the serious stretching. A 7-foot square trestle table was the stage, the two brothers, dressed in bakers'

3

whites, the skilled performers. With fingers curved under, Mike placed a disk of dough on his knuckles, then stretched it by flipping and turning the disk, letting the dough expand under its own weight. As one catching the gold ring on a merry-go-round, Mihran caught the opposite side of the dough, and the brothers worked in unison, flipping, twisting, and stretching.

As the dough grew in size, the brothers moved farther apart, until they were at opposite corners of the table. The only sound was a dull *flap, flap*. As the dough became thinner, the sound became *swish, swish*. In less than a minute the disk was a 7-foot square. One final dusting of cornstarch, one final billowing stretch, and the dough floated to the table like a parachute. As each sheet was made it was stacked upon the last one, then the treasure of filo was covered with a heavy canvas sheet until it was time for cutting into smaller units. The filo maker as well as the filo cook needs to protect the parchment-thin dough from air.

Filo making by hand is a laborious, no longer profitable art. To make 100 pounds of filo took the Sagatelyans 9 to 10 hours. It's no wonder Migirdich Sagatelyan predicts that before too long filo will be made exclusively by machine.

Cooking with Filo

Machine-made filo tastes the same as the handmade product, and because it comes in neat rectangles it is even easier to use. Buying machine-made dough leaves you more time for the fun of turning filo into fabulous appetizers, entrées, and desserts.

If you have never worked with filo, the next few pages are intended for you. If you are an old filo hand eager to rediscover its many uses, you may prefer to turn directly to the recipes. Some of the filo-wrapped dishes are as glittering as diamonds from Tiffany's, some as practical as T-shirts from Sears. May they bring you great pleasure at the table.

Buying Filo

Filo, the Greek word for leaf, has many equivalents: *fila, phyllo, phylla, fillo*, and *strudel leaves*. Available under any of these names in imported food shops, Middle Eastern markets, and many supermarkets, filo is sold ready to use, fresh or frozen, in 1-pound boxes.

Each box contains about 24 sheets of dough that measure approximately 12 inches x 17 inches or 14 inches x 18 inches, depending on the manufacturer. In some areas pre-buttered filo is available, in whole sheets or 4 inch x 12 inch strips suitable for small rolls and triangles.

Storing Filo

You may not use filo daily, but if it's stored in the freezer, you may not use it at all. You'll be more inclined to work with filo when the dough is refrigerated and ready to go.

Thaw frozen filo, still in the unopened package, in the refrigerator. Thawing takes about 8 hours. Don't be tempted to thaw the filo at room temperature. Rapid thawing creates moisture and may cause the sheets to stick together.

Fresh or thawed filo has a storage life in the refrigerator of 3 to 4 weeks. Spots of mold, such as you would find on bread, indicate the filo is past its prime and should be discarded.

For easiest handling, let the unopened filo stand at room temperature (not over 80°F) for at least 1 hour before using it. This makes it more supple. (As long as it is protected from air, it cannot spoil). After opening a box of filo, you don't need to use it all. Place the unused sheets in a sealable plastic bag, and refrigerate them until your next project.

Butter and Oils for Filo

As filo is layered it must be brushed with some type of fat to give it flavor and to make it crisp. For savory dishes, regular butter is suitable. For sweet pastries, many cooks prefer unsalted butter. Melt the butter in a bowl in a microwave oven or in a small pan over low heat, being careful that it does not brown.

Clarified butter works extremely well with filo. To clarify butter, melt 1 cup butter in a small pan over low heat. As the milky foam rises, skim it off and discard it. Pour off the clear, golden melted butter, discarding the white milk solids at the bottom of the pan. This makes about ¼ cup clarified butter. Store it in the refrigerator for up to 2 weeks.

Most recipes in this book call for butter for brushing filo. If for dietary reasons you prefer to use margarine, the textural result, though not the flavor, will be the same. Avoid using whipped diet butter and diet margarine that contains water.

For some savory dishes, oil can replace butter, or you can combine butter and oil. It's a matter of taste. Olive oil lends a delicious flavor, as do almond oil, avocado oil, and walnut oil. Use the stronger-flavored oils—hazelnut oil, sesame oil, and chili oil —in small amounts combined with butter or a vegetable oil.

Use a sparing hand when you brush filo with butter; use no more than 2 teaspoons per sheet. You don't need to cover the whole sheet. Just brush a few streaks, lay on the next sheet, and brush again, changing the direction of the streaks.

Filo Tools

You can work with filo on your kitchen counter, but I find it easier to work on a large plastic cutting board, which won't be damaged when I cut filo strips or circles. Turn the board if you decide to change direction in folding; it's easier than turning a stack of filled filo.

For brushing butter, use a natural-bristle paintbrush or pastry brush 1½ to 2½ inches wide. A smaller brush is good for brushing crinkled edges.

To cut filo, use the tip of a sharp knife. A ruler may help you cut straight edges at first, but you'll soon learn to eyeball it.

A water mister, though not essential, is handy to resurrect sheets of filo that have become too dry. If you wish, spray a light mist of water on filo pie crusts before baking to make them extra crisp.

To protect filo from air, I find it easiest to sandwich the sheets between two clean dish towels. If the day is very warm, it's good insurance to place one damp (not wet) towel under the bottom dry towel, and another damp towel over the top dry towel.

Filo Shapes

You'll find folding directions throughout this book, with suggested sizes and dimensions. Please remember they are only suggestions. The size of filo sheets varies with the manufacturer and there is always more than one way to wrap filo. If a recipe says to make a small triangle and it suits your purpose to make a large one, adjust the size of the filo strips and increase the amount of the filling.

Filo Toppings

There are many things you can sprinkle on a filo package to enhance flavor and appearance. Very finely ground nuts are good on sweet pastries, and grated Parmesan cheese on savory ones. Seeds, such as caraway, poppy, black mustard, and black and white sesame seeds, work well. Dried herbs tend to darken in baking, but ground red chili, chili powder, and paprika add a dash of color.

Storing Filled Filo

Most filo pastries in this book can be covered and refrigerated until you are ready to use them. As a rule of thumb, pastries with cooked fillings, such as Chimichangas and Jambalaya Rolls, can be held up to 24 hours. Fillings that contain uncooked poultry, fish, meat, or eggs should be baked within 8 hours.

You can freeze most filled pastries unbaked. Small pastries can go from freezer to oven without thawing, but you need to increase the baking time. Remove from the freezer large pies, such as those assembled in a 9 x 13inch pan, 30 minutes to 1 hour before baking.

Baking and Reheating Filo

Always bake filo uncovered so it will brown and crisp. Oven temperatures frequently vary from the settings, so the best way of judging when the pastry is done is by color. In most cases fully baked filo will be golden brown. If, for example, you bake a triangle with a very moist filling, the ends of the triangle will brown while the center will remain a lighter color.

To reheat filo pastries, bake them in a 200° to 250°F. conventional oven—never a microwave oven—until heated through. If the tops of the pastries brown before the filling gets hot, cover the pastries loosely with a piece of foil.

Before You Start

Assemble everything you need before you open the package of filo. Clear off the counter, prepare your filling, melt the butter, and set out the covering towels. If you are not quite certain how you want to fold the filo, practice with a piece of tissue paper. It will soon become second nature.

Frequent Filo Questions

There is a white powder on my filo. Is is still good to use?

The powder is cornstarch, which the manufacturer sprinkles over the sheets before stacking them. It prevents the layers from sticking together, and it does not affect the flavor.

The edges of my filo are dry and cracked. Should I throw the whole package away?

When it's not protected from air, filo dries out, starting at the edges and progressing toward the center of the sheet. Trim the edges and work with smaller-size sheets, being sure to keep the unused sheets covered.

I covered the filo with a damp towel, and now the sheets stick together. What should I do?

Don't try to separate them. Treat them as one sheet, brush with butter, and continue with the next sheet. To prevent sticking, place unused filo between two dry towels, then place a damp towel under and over the stack.

When I stack the buttered sheets of filo, sometimes I get wrinkles. If I try to separate the buttered sheets, they break or tear. What should I do?

If you get wrinkles, just press them down flat. They'll never show when the filo is folded into a triangle or other shape, or when it is layered in a pie. If you get a tear, patch it with a small piece of filo if you wish, or overlook the tear and cover it with a new sheet of filo.

I hate to waste filo. What do I do with the trimmings when I cut it into a circle or other fancy shape?

Make filo flakes (page 81). They can be used for coatings, fillers, and toppings—the same ways you use dry bread crumbs.

My filo pastries aren't flaky, and they look greasy. How do I correct this?

Use a light hand when brushing filo with butter or oil. Too much fat makes filo soggy rather than crisp. Two teaspoons of butter or oil is the maximum amount you need for each sheet. For lighter pastries, use 1 teaspoon per sheet.

My baklava *looked beautiful when it came from the oven. After I poured the hot syrup over it, it became soggy. What happened?*

When you pour syrup over filo pastries such as *baklava*, *bourma*, or nightingale's nests, it is essential to have the temperature of the syrup and pastry at opposite extremes. Pour cool syrup over hot pastry or hot syrup over cool pastry to achieve a crisp, still moist sweet.

What can I do to prevent baked filo from shattering when I cut it?

Use a serrated knife, such as a bread knife, and cut with a sawing motion.

Won't I get fat by eating all that filo?

By itself, filo is low in calories. One ounce, approximately 1⅓ sheets, contains 80 calories, 3 grams of protein, 18 grams of carbohydrate, 100 milligrams of sodium, and no fat or cholesterol. When you spread butter or oil on filo you add calories and fat, but the number of calories in filo pastry is much lower than that in pie pastry or puff pastry.

Eating more calories than you burn is what pushes up the pounds. Enjoy the sweets in small portions, and remember that you can create a dramatic and flavorful entrée with only one or two sheets of filo and a tablespoon of butter.

I watch my cholesterol. Can I brush filo with something other than butter?

Definitely. Margarine can be used in place of butter, but avoid using whipped diet spreads, which contain water. For savory dishes, olive oil is a good choice. All fats and oils make filo crisp, so it's a matter of personal taste.

When I cook ahead, is it better to freeze filo before or after it's baked?

Either method will work. For the freshest taste, most cooks prefer to freeze filo unbaked and bake it as needed.

2
Appetizers

Appetizer Triangles

For a stand-up appetizer party, filo folded into tiny triangles is an ideal choice. The crisp, multilayered puffs are easy to serve and tidy to eat. Best of all, they freeze beautifully unbaked, so when it's party time, you can pull out just the number and variety you want for a fresh-from-the-oven hot hors d'oeuvre.

To shape the triangles, lay a sheet of filo horizontally on your work surface, and brush it lightly with melted butter (about 2 teaspoons). Lay another sheet of filo over the first, and brush it with butter. Cut the filo crosswise into five equal strips about 3 inches wide and 12 inches long. Place a rounded teaspoon of filling on one end of each strip. Fold over one corner to make a triangle. Fold the triangle over again on itself. Continue folding, from one side to the other, as if you were folding a flag. When you come to the end of a strip, if there is a little piece of filo too narrow to be tucked under, trim it off with a knife.

After folding five triangles, place them on an ungreased baking sheet and butter the tops. You can leave the tops plain if you use only one kind of filling, but if you wrap a variety of fillings, identify each kind with a topping such as poppy seeds or sesame seeds. Surprises are fun, but not everyone likes or can tolerate the same foods, so when you serve a tray of assorted appetizers at a later date, you want to be able to let guests know what's inside. I don't trust my memory: I write the code, such as "Parmesan cheese—mushroom triangles," on a piece of paper and pack it with the appetizers when I freeze them.

After folding the appetizers, cover and chill them if you are going to use them within 24 hours. For longer storage, freeze them solid on the baking sheet, then transfer them to containers with tight-fitting lids and return them to the freezer.

Bake the triangles, uncovered, in a pre-heated 350°F. oven for 15 minutes (20 to 25 minutes if frozen) or until they are golden brown.

On the following eight pages is a selection of some of my favorite fillings for appetizer triangles. Some are traditional, some break with tradition, and some are spur-of-the-moment creations too good to forget. Once you get started, you'll discover the fun of creating your own fillings from bits of leftover meat, fish, or cheese. To make 20 appetizer triangles, you'll need eight sheets of filo and a scant cup of filling. Taste the filling before you wrap it up. Does it need additional seasoning? If it tastes good in the mixing bowl, you know it will be a winner wrapped in filo.

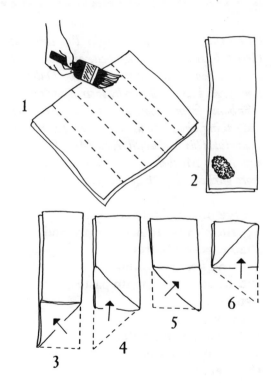

Kreatopetes

Of all the savory meat triangles I've eaten at Greek church bazaars, the best, and the one I use as a benchmark, comes from the Dalienes family. As kids, we'd stop by their house on the way home from school, and if Mary's mother was baking, she's shoo us out of the kitchen with a plateful of her wonderful treats. Mary Dalienes, now Mary Mitchel, says her kreatopetes *are more garlicky than those she grew up with.*

1 large onion, finely chopped
4 garlic cloves , minced or pressed
2 tablespoons butter
1 pound ground round
1 (6-ounce) can tomato paste
1 cup water
1 teaspoon salt
1 teaspoon ground allspice
$^{1}/_{2}$ teaspoon ground black pepper
18 sheets filo
¾ cup butter, melted, for brushing filo

In a wide frying pan over medium heat, cook the onion and garlic in the 2 tablespoons butter until the onion is limp. Crumble in the beef; cook until it is browned. Drain off and discard the drippings.

In a bowl, whisk together the tomato paste, water, salt, allspice, and pepper until smooth. Stir this mixture into the meat mixture. Cover the pan, and simmer for 30 minutes. Remove the cover, and cook the mixture briefly, until it is thick and the liquid has evaporated. Remove the pan from the heat, and let the mixture cool.

Using a rounded teaspoon of filling for each, fill, fold, and bake the triangles as explained on page 5, 12, and 13.

Yield: About 45 appetizers

Mushroom Triangles

This creamy filling tastes similar to a mushroom pâté. If you don't have a food processor to chop the mushrooms, use a chef's knife.

½ pound mushrooms, finely chopped
2 green onions (including tops), finely chopped
2 tablespoons butter
2 tablespoons vermouth or dry white wine
1 (8-ounce) package cream cheese, softened
2 tablespoons grated Parmesan cheese
2 tablespoons minced fresh dill, or 2 teaspoons dried dill weed
Salt and pepper to taste
16 sheets filo
⅔ cup butter, melted, for brushing filo
Grated Parmesan cheese for topping

In a wide frying pan over medium heat, cook the mushrooms and green onions in the 2 tablespoons butter for 3 minutes. Add the vermouth, and increase the heat to medium-high. Cook 5 or 6 minutes, or until the pan juices have evaporated. Remove the pan from the heat, and let the mixture cool.

In a bowl, beat together the cream cheese, the 2 tablespoons Parmesan cheese, and the dill until smooth. Stir in the mushrooms and the salt and pepper. Using a rounded teaspoon of filling for each, fill, fold, and bake the triangles as explained on page 13. After buttering the tops of the triangles, sprinkle them with Parmesan cheese.

Yield: About 40 appetizers

Curried Shrimp Puffs

With no cooking involved, this filling goes together in minutes.

1 (8-ounce) package cream cheese, softened
1 egg yolk
2 teaspoons lemon juice
1 teaspoon curry powder
¾ pound small cooked shrimp, finely chopped
2 green onions (including tops), finely chopped
20 sheets filo
⅞ cup butter, melted, for brushing filo
Black mustard seeds or sesame seeds for topping

In a bowl, beat together the cream cheese, egg yolk, lemon juice, and curry powder until smooth. Stir in the shrimp and green onions. Using a rounded teaspoon for each, fill, fold, and bake the triangles as explained on page 12 and 13. After buttering the tops of the triangles, sprinkle each with a few mustard seeds or sesame seeds.

Yield: About 50 appetizers

Chicken Liver Triangles

Like any filling made with cream cheese, this one is easier to work with if it has not been chilled. Place a mound of the filling on the filo, fold over one corner to make a triangle, and press lightly before continuing to fold. This light pressure spreads the pâté evenly inside the packet.

2 green onions (including tops), finely
   chopped
1 garlic clove, minced or pressed
2 tablespoons butter
¾ pound chicken livers, cut in half
1 tablespoon brandy
1 tablespoon chopped parsley
¼ teaspoon dried thyme leaves
1 (8-ounce) package cream cheese,
   softened
Salt and pepper to taste
20 sheets filo
⅞ cup butter, melted, for brushing filo
Poppy seeds for topping

In a wide frying pan over medium-high heat, cook the green onions and garlic in the 2 tablespoons butter for 30 seconds. Add the livers, and cook for 5 minutes. Add the brandy and parsley, and cook 2 minutes more, or until the pan juices have evaporated and the livers are no longer pink inside when cut. Stir in the thyme and let the mixture cool.

In a food processor, process the cream cheese until smooth. Add the livers, and process briefly to make a coarse purée. Add salt and pepper.

Using a rounded teaspoon for each, fill, fold, and bake the triangles as explained on page 12 and 13. After buttering the tops of the triangles, sprinkle each with a few poppy seeds.

Yield: About 50 appetizers

Sambusik

Lamb is the traditional filling in this Lebanese appetizer, but it tastes equally good made with beef. Regular ground meat makes a rather coarse, crumbly mixture that spills out from the first fold of the triangle, so to expedite filling, I whirl the cooked meat briefly in a food processor before adding the pine nuts.

¼ cup whole pine nuts
2 tablespoons butter
1 small onion, finely chopped
1 pound lean ground lamb or
    ground beef
½ teaspoon salt
½ teaspoon ground allspice
¼ teaspoon ground black pepper
14 sheets filo
⅔ cup butter, melted, for brushing filo
Finely chopped pine nuts for topping

In a wide frying pan over low heat, cook the whole pine nuts in the 2 tablespoons butter, stirring frequently, until they are lightly browned. Lift them out with a slotted spoon, and set them aside.

Increase the heat to medium. Add the onion, and cook it until it is soft. Crumble in the meat and cook it, stirring occasionally, until it is well browned. Drain off and discard the pan drippings. Stir in the salt, allspice, and pepper, and let the mixture cool. In a food processor, process the mixture until it is finely chopped but not puréed. Stir in the toasted nuts.

Using a rounded teaspoon of filling for each, fill, fold, and bake the triangles as explained on page 12 and 13. After buttering the tops of the triangles, sprinkle them with chopped pine nuts.

Yield: About 35 appetizers

Santa Fe Triangles

I'm such a fan of Southwestern flavors, I couldn't wait to bake these to see how they tasted. Muy bueno! Use refried black beans or refried pinto beans, homemade or canned. Resist any temptation to add more beans. Too high a proportion of beans creates steam, which prevents the filo from browning evenly.

½ cup refried beans
2 tablespoons canned diced green
  chiles
1 cup (4 ounces) shredded jack cheese
About 30 cilantro leaves
12 sheets filo
½ cup butter, melted, for brushing filo
Mild ground red chili or chili powder
  for topping

In a bowl, combine the refried beans, green chiles, and cheese; mix well.

Using a rounded teaspoon of filling and one cilantro leaf for each, fill, fold, and bake the triangles as directed on page 12 and 13. After buttering the tops of the triangles, sprinkle them with ground chili.

Yield: About 30 appetizers

Shrimp or Crab Pillows

Everyone loves shrimp toast, but I don't enjoy deep frying the toasts when I am entertaining guests. The solution is to wrap the filling in filo for an appetizer that bakes unattended.

1 egg white
2 teaspoons cornstarch mixed with
    2 teaspoons dry sherry
1 teaspoon minced fresh ginger
½ teaspoon salt
¾ pound medium raw shrimp, shelled,
    deveined, and finely chopped or 1 ¼
    cups cooked or canned crab meat,
    flaked and pressed dry between
    paper towels
¼ cup water chestnuts, finely chopped
1 tablespoon chopped cilantro
12 sheets filo
⅓ cup butter, melted, mixed with
    2 teaspoons sesame oil, for brushing
    filo
Sesame seeds for topping

In a bowl, beat the egg white until foamy. Whisk in the cornstarch-sherry mixture, ginger, and salt. Stir in the shrimp or crab, water chestnuts, and cilantro. Chill the filling for 30 minutes.

Using a rounded teaspoon for each triangle, fill and fold the triangles as explained on page 12 and 13. Use the butter-sesame oil mixture to brush the filo strips and the tops of the triangles, and sprinkle each triangle with a few sesame seeds. Cover and chill the triangles up to 4 hours.

Preheat the oven to 375°F. Bake the triangles, uncovered, for 18 to 20 minutes, or until they are puffed and golden.

These pillows do not freeze well, but you can chill them up to four hours before baking.

Yield: About 30 appetizers

Samosas

In another break with tradition, filo stands in for dough wrappers in light, crisp Indian samosas made without the fuss of deep frying.

1 medium onion, chopped
2 garlic cloves, minced or pressed
1 teaspoon minced fresh ginger
1 tablespoon vegetable oil
½ pound ground round
1 *jalapeño* or *serrano* chile, seeded and minced
1 teaspoon curry powder
½ cup canned tomatoes, drained and finely chopped
1 2-inch thin-skinned potato, boiled, peeled, and shredded
1 tablespoon lemon juice
½ teaspoon salt
2 tablespoons chopped cilantro
16 sheets filo
⅔ cup butter, melted, for brushing filo

In a wide frying pan over medium heat, cook the onion, garlic, and ginger in the oil until the onion is soft. Crumble in the beef, and add the chile. Cook until the meat is well browned. Drain off and discard the drippings. Add the curry powder and tomatoes. Cook for 2 minutes. Add the potato, lemon juice, and salt. Cook over low heat until all the liquid is absorbed. Stir in the cilantro, and let the mixture cool.

Using a rounded teaspoon of filling for each triangle, fill, fold, and bake the triangles as explained on page 12 and 13.

Yield: About 40 appetizers

Rolled Appetizers

Another way of folding filo for appetizers is like a miniature jelly roll with the sides folded in first. There are many variations on this theme, from Greek *bourekakia* to Turkish *borek* to Armenian *boerags*. You can make these cigar-size pastries with any of the appetizer triangle fillings. For each small roll, use ⅓ sheet of filo — a strip 5 to 6 inches wide and about 12 inches long. Brush the strip with melted butter. Spread a rounded teaspoon of filling in a band along the short edge of the filo closest to you, 1 inch from the bottom; leave a 1-inch margin at either side. Fold the bottom edge over the filling. Fold in the sides. Roll up the filo jelly-roll style.

When you cook for a crowd, it's faster to make long rolls and cut them into bite-size pieces after baking. Like appetizer triangles, long rolls freeze well, with one added advantage: their compact shape takes up little freezer space. If your freezer is as filled as mine, you know it's important to think about storage logistics when planning a large affair. Be sure to offer napkins when you serve these slices. With ends open, they are not quite as tidy to eat as triangles or individual rolls.

To make long rolls, stack three sheets of filo horizontally on your work surface, brushing each sheet lightly with melted butter (about 2 teaspoons) as you stack. Spoon the filling in a band along the long edge of the filo closest to you, 2 inches from the bottom edge and 1 inch from the sides. Fold the bottom edge over the filling. Fold in the sides. Roll up the filo jelly-roll style. Cut the roll in half.

Place the rolls, seam side down, on an ungreased baking sheet. Brush them with butter. Cover and chill them if you plan to bake them within 24 hours. For longer storage, freeze them solid on the baking sheet, then transfer them to sealable plastic bags and return them to the freezer.

Preheat the oven to 375°F. Bake the rolls, uncovered, for 20 minutes (25 minutes if frozen), or until they are lightly browned. Let long rolls cool for 5 minutes before slicing them. With a heavy chef's knife, trim the ends, then cut the rolls into 1-inch pieces.

long roll

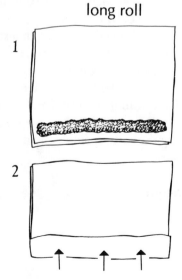

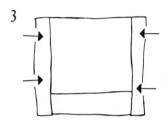

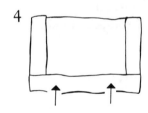

Dutch Treats

One of the most popular appetizers from my catering days, this roll pairs the sweetness of slow-cooked onions with the sweet, nutty flavor of Gouda cheese, all wrapped in buttery filo.

2 tablespoons butter
3 medium onions, very thinly sliced
1 (3-ounce) package cream cheese, softened
1 teaspoon Dijon mustard
¼ teaspoon caraway seeds
1 cup (4 ounces) shredded Gouda cheese
6 sheets filo
4 tablespoons butter, melted, for brushing filo
Caraway seeds for topping

Melt the 2 tablespoons butter in a wide frying pan over medium-low heat. Add the onions and stir to coat them with butter. Cover the pan, and cook the onions, stirring occasionally, for 20 minutes or until they are limp. Add a few drops of water if the pan becomes dry. Uncover the pan, and continue to cook, stirring often, until the onions are soft and golden, about 20 minutes more. Let the onions cool.

In a bowl, combine the cream cheese, mustard, and the ¼ teaspoon caraway seeds. Stir in the Gouda cheese and onions.

Make two long rolls, using 3 sheets of filo and half the filling for each. Fill, roll, and bake the rolls as explained on page 23. After buttering the rolls, sprinkle them with a few caraway seeds.

Yield: About 28 appetizers

Caramelized Onion Rolls

If you like blue-veined cheese with a bold, earthy flavor, use Gorgonzola or Roquefort. For a less pungent flavor, choose one of the American or Scandinavian blues.

1 tablespoon each butter and olive oil
3 medium onions, very thinly sliced
1 (3-ounce) package cream cheese, softened
½ cup (3 ounces) crumbled blue-veined cheese
¼ teaspoon dried rosemary, crumbled
⅛ teaspoon ground black pepper
6 sheets filo
2 tablespoons each melted butter and olive oil, mixed, for brushing filo

Melt the 1 tablespoon butter with the 1 tablespoon olive oil in a wide frying pan over medium-low heat. Add the onions and stir to coat them. Cover the pan and cook the onions, stirring occasionally for 20 minutes, or until they are limp. Add a few drops of water if the pan becomes dry. Uncover the pan and continue to cook, stirring often, until the onions are soft and golden, about 20 minutes more. Let the onions cool.

In a bowl, combine the cream cheese, blue cheese, rosemary, and pepper. Stir in the onions. Make two long rolls, using 3 sheets of filo and half the filling for each. Fill, roll, and bake the rolls as explained on page 23, brushing the filo with the butter-oil mixture.

Yield: About 28 appetizers

Crinkled Cups

Unlike other filo appetizers, which are wrapped around a filling and baked, crinkled cups are bite-size filo shells that are baked "blind" (empty) and filled before serving. If you fill them with a cold mixture, they can be passed as finger food. If the filling is hot, serve them on plates. For an interesting first course, serve each person three cups, with a different cold filling in each, and garnish with fresh herbs or edible flowers.

Crinkled cups take more time to make than plain shells (page 119), but they look so pretty, I think they are worth it. This style of filo folding looks complicated. The truth is, you can do it in minutes. The trick is to keep unused filo sheets protected from air; if the filo becomes dry, it will crumble rather than crinkle. To crinkle the dough, you need a 15- to 20-inch length of ¼-inch wooden dowel, or a long cooking chopstick. Before you begin, melt butter for brushing the filo and beat an egg in a small bowl.

Place both within reach.

To make the cups, use one sheet of filo for every two cups desired. Cut the filo in half to make rectangles about 8 by 12 inches. Place one half sheet on your work surface; cover the unused filo with a towel to prevent it from drying. Brush the filo with 1 teaspoon melted butter. Fold it in half to make a rectangle about 4 by 12 inches. Brush the top lightly with butter. Lay the dowel or chopstick along the folded edge. Holding the filo against the dowel, roll the filo loosely onto the dowel to about ½ inch of the opposite edge. Gently push both ends of the filo along the dowel toward the center, until the filo is crinkled and about 3½ inches long. Holding the filo, pull out the dowel.

With the free edge of the filo toward the center, curve the crinkled roll to make a cup. The free edge becomes the bottom of the cup; the crinkled filo forms the sides.

Overlap the ends, moisten them with egg, and press to seal them. Place the cup in an ungreased baking pan, and brush it lightly with butter. Repeat this process to make as many cups as you need.

Preheat the oven to 350 °F. Bake the cups, uncovered, for 15 minutes, or until they are golden brown. Place the pan on a rack and let the cups cool. Store them in an airtight container up to three days, or freeze them. If the cups have lost a little crispness during storage, heat them in a 200°F. oven for 5 minutes a few hours before filling.

How far in advance of serving can you fill the cups? It depends upon the filling. Moisture and lengthy refrigeration wilt even the flakiest filo, so when I use a slightly wet filling or one that requires refrigeration, I fill the cups close to serving time. Any hot filling should be added just before serving.

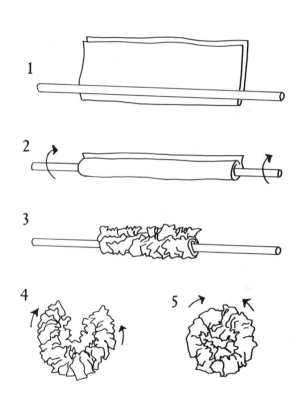

Smoked Salmon Cups

Some food combinations are just too good to change. Lox and cream cheese are perfect on bagels for brunch. For glittering party food, filo cups make more stylish containers.

1 (3-ounce) package cream cheese, softened
2 tablespoons sour cream
1 tablespoon minced fresh dill
1 (3-ounce) package lox or other cold-smoked salmon, thinly sliced
12 crinkled cups (page 27)
Dill sprigs for garnish

In a bowl, blend the cream cheese, sour cream, and dill until smooth. Refrigerate the mixture, covered, until you are ready to use it. Cut the salmon lengthwise into ½-inch-wide strips. Roll up each strip, overlapping short strips if necessary, then open one end slightly so it resembles a flower. Place the rolled strips on a plate, cover them, and chill until you are ready to use them.

To assemble, place about 2 teaspoons of the cream cheese mixture in each crinkled cup. Garnish each with a roll of salmon and a sprig of dill. Serve the cups at once or chill them up to 1 hour.

Yield: 12 appetizers

Caviar Cups

This recipe, so simple it has no proportions, makes a stunning appetizer to serve with champagne.

Shortly before serving, place a heaping teaspoon of sour cream in each crinkled cup (page 27). Spread the sour cream evenly over the center of the cup with the back of a spoon. Top each cup with about 1/2 teaspoon caviar, then sprinkle with a few minced chives.

Caviar comes in a wide range of prices, so let your pocketbook be your guide. Middle-priced red salmon caviar and golden whitefish caviar are naturally colored and can be spooned right from the jar. To complement a black and white theme one New Year's Eve, I used lumpfish caviar dyed black to simulate more expensive types; it also is dyed red. To reduce the salt and dye content, rinse dyed caviar in a fine wire strainer with cold running water until the water runs out fairly clear, 2 to 3 minutes. Drain the caviar, then cover and chill it until you are ready to use it.

Chèvre Cups

Simplicity is key to the elegance of this warm appetizer.

¼ cup virgin olive oil
1 garlic clove, peeled and crushed
3 sprigs fresh thyme, or ½ teaspoon
   dried thyme leaves
2 sprigs fresh rosemary, or ¼ teaspoon
   dried rosemary leaves
1 (6-ounce) log goat cheese (chèvre)
12 crinkled cups (page 27)

In a wide shallow bowl, combine the olive oil, garlic, thyme, and rosemary. Cut the goat cheese into six slices, place the slices in the bowl, and turn them to coat all sides. Cover the bowl and chill for 8 hours.

Lift the cheese from the oil, drain it briefly, and cut each slice in half. Place one piece in each filo cup. Place the cups in a baking pan, cover them, and chill them up to 4 hours.

Preheat the oven to 350°F. Bake the cups, uncovered, until they are just heated through, about 5 minutes.

Yield: 12 appetizers

Smoked Fish Cups

Esther Walkenshaw makes a mouth-watering smoked fish spread for crackers. I serve her spread in filo shells and love it even more.

1 (8-ounce) package cream cheese, softened
2 tablespoons light cream
½ cup finely chopped walnuts
2 tablespoons chopped parsley
2 tablespoons chopped green onion
2 teaspoons lemon juice
1 can (about 3 ½ ounces) smoked sturgeon, smoked albacore, or smoked salmon, flaked
4 dozen crinkled cups (page 27) or tartlet shells (page 120)

In a bowl, beat the cream cheese and cream until smooth. Stir in the walnuts, parsley, green onion, and lemon juice. Add the fish, and mix lightly. Cover and chill the filling until you are ready to use it.

To assemble the appetizers, mound a heaping teaspoon of filling in each filo cup. Serve the cups at once, or chill them up to 1 hour.

Yield: 4 dozen appetizers

Liptauer Cups

Liptauer cheese spread is an old favorite that has never gone out of style. It gains a fresh look when you serve it in filo cups. If you make the filling ahead, let it soften at room temperature for 30 minutes before filling the cups.

1 (8-ounce) package cream cheese, softened
4 tablespoons butter, softened
¼ cup sour cream
1 teaspoon Dijon mustard
1 teaspoon paprika
1 teaspoon caraway seeds
1 teaspoon anchovy paste
2 green onions (including tops), finely chopped
2 teaspoons capers, rinsed and chopped
4 dozen crinkled cups (page 27) or tartlet shells (page 120)
Shredded red radishes for garnish (optional)

Combine the cream cheese, butter, sour cream, Dijon mustard, paprika, caraway seeds, and anchovy paste in a large bowl. Blend until the mixture is smooth. Stir in the green onions and capers. Cover and chill the filling until you are ready to use it.

To assemble the cups, mound a heaping teaspoon of filling in each filo cup. If desired, sprinkle each with a few radish shreds. Serve the cups at once, or chill them up to 1 hour.

Yield: 4 dozen appetizers

Tartaletas

Every country includes little dishes, or snacks, in its culinary repertoire, and Spain is no exception. There you will find tartlets such as these offered as part of a tapas *selection. Tartaletas make a splendid light appetizer, accompanied by a glass of Spanish sherry.*

1 (6 ½-ounce) can solid white tuna
2 tablespoons mayonnaise
2 teaspoons red wine vinegar
2 teaspoons capers, rinsed and
  chopped
2 green onions (including tops), finely
  chopped
1 tablepoon minced parsley
16 tartlet shells (page 120)
Diced pimiento for garnish

Drain the tuna; flake it into a bowl. Add the mayonnaise, wine vinegar, capers, green onions, and parsley. Mix well. Cover and chill the filling until you are ready to use it.

To assemble the tartaletas, mound a spoonful of tuna mixture in each tartlet shell. Garnish each with a piece of pimiento. Serve the tartaletas at once, or chill them up to 1 hour.

Yield: 16 appetizers

Filo-Wrapped Brie

I would never advise tampering with a perfectly ripened Brie, but sometimes you may need to serve one before it has had time to fully mature. To give it new life as well as a little flair, filo-wrap a young Brie—one that is firm when you cut a slit in the center—and bake it. Spread the warm cheese on slices of French bread, accompanied by grapes and sliced pears or apples. A chilled Johannesburg riesling would be a fine choice for wine.

4 sheets filo
3 tablespoons butter, melted, for brushing filo
2 tablespoons sliced almonds or chopped pecans
1 6- or 7-ounce whole Brie or Camembert round, with rind

Trim the filo to make 12-inch squares. Stack the squares, brushing each lightly with the melted butter as you stack. Sprinkle the nuts in the center of the stack in a circle about the size of the cheese round. Place the cheese over the nuts. Fold one corner of the filo over the cheese as illustrated on the facing page, and brush with a little butter. Fold over the rest of the corners, one by one, brushing with a little butter after each fold. Press the filo against the cheese to make a smooth package. Place the wrapped cheese seam side down on an ungreased baking sheet. Brush the top lightly with butter. Cover and chill the wrapped cheese until you are ready to bake it.

Preheat the oven to 350°F. Bake the wrapped cheese, uncovered, for 20 minutes, or until the filo is golden brown. Let it cool for about 10 minutes before serving.

Yield: 6 servings

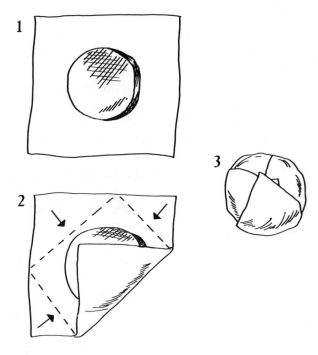

Scallops and Pesto Packets

Brimming with the flavors of summer, this is a colorful starter for a main-dish soup or salad meal. When I tested this recipe, my goal was to bake the appetizers long enough to brown the filo without overcooking the scallops. Small bay scallops were disappointingly tough, but large whole sea scallops were perfect—tender and juicy. You can use canned roasted red peppers and a good quality purchased pesto that is not too oily.

Pesto
¾ cup packed fresh basil leaves
⅓ cup grated Parmesan cheese
1 small garlic clove, minced or pressed
3 tablespoons olive oil
1 teaspoon lemon juice

Red Pepper Sauce
1 large red bell pepper or 1 cup canned
  roasted red bell pepper, drained
1 medium tomato, peeled, seeded,
  diced

½ cup chicken broth
¼ cup dry white wine
1 teaspoon olive oil
½ teaspoon lemon juice

¾ pound whole sea scallops
¼ teaspoon salt
6 sheets filo
2 tablespoons each melted butter and
  olive oil, mixed, for brushing filo
Fresh basil leaves for garnish

For the pesto, process the basil, cheese, garlic, olive oil, and lemon juice in a blender or food processor until smooth. Transfer the pesto to a bowl, and chill it until you need it.

For the sauce, place the whole bell pepper, if you are using a fresh one, in a pan. Broil it 2 inches from the heat, turning frequently, until the pepper is lightly charred on all sides. Place the pepper in a plastic bag, and close the bag tightly. Let the pepper sweat 15 minutes to loosen its skin. Peel the pepper; discard the skin, seeds, and pith. Coarsely chop the pepper .

In a 2-quart pan, simmer the chopped pepper, tomato, chicken broth, and wine, covered, for 10 minutes. Uncover the pan, and continue to simmer the sauce until two-thirds of the liquid has evaporated. In a food processor or blender, purée the sauce until smooth. Return it to the pan, and stir in the olive oil and lemon juice. If you are making it ahead, cover and chill it.

Pat the scallops dry with paper towels. Place them in a bowl with the pesto and salt. Stir to distribute the seasonings.

Place one sheet of filo horizontally on your work surface. Lightly brush the right half with the butter-oil mixture. Fold the left half over the buttered right side and brush with the butter-oil mixture again. Place ⅙ of the scallops along the edge nearest you, 2 inches from the edge; leave a 2-inch margin on either side. Fold the bottom edge over the filling. Fold in the sides. Fold the filo completely, from bottom to top, to make a packet about 4 inches by 2 inches. Place the packet seam side down in an ungreased baking pan, and brush with the butter-oil mixture. Repeat the process to make five more packets. If you are making the packets ahead, cover and chill them up to 2 hours.

Preheat the oven to 400°F. Bake the packets, uncovered, for 8 minutes (10 minutes if they have been refrigerated) or until the ends of the packets are golden brown and the centers are crisp and light brown. Reheat the red pepper sauce. Place one appetizer on each serving plate. Spoon the sauce over the centers of the packets, and garnish each with a basil leaf.

Yield: 6 first-course appetizers

Warm Chèvre, Fig, and Walnut Tartlets

Abby Nash, chef-owner of the popular Abby's in Ithaca, New York, created this unusual and delicious first course. He makes filo shells in 4 ½-inch tart pans. (If you don't have this size pan, see page 119 for other suggestions.) To complement this starter, he suggests a glass of the same wine used for poaching the figs.

10 sheets filo
4 tablespoons unsalted butter, melted
8 dried figs, preferably Calimyrna
½ cup sweet riesling or
   gewürztraminer wine
1 teaspoon honey
6 ounces goat cheese (chèvre)
¼ cup ricotta cheese, puréed
¼ cup toasted walnuts, coarsely
   chopped

Preheat the oven to 350°F. Stack five sheets of filo, brushing each sheet lightly with butter as you stack. Using the tip of a sharp knife and a small plate or bowl as a guide, cut out two 7-inch circles of filo and place each in a 4 ½-inch tart pan. With a fork, prick the dough in the bottoms of the pans. Repeat this process to make two more tart shells. Bake the shells 10 to 15 minutes, or until they are golden brown.

Combine the figs, wine, and honey in a small saucepan. Simmer, uncovered, until the figs are tender and the liquid has been absorbed. Let the figs cool, then remove their stems and cut each fig into six pieces.

Mix the cheeses. Divide the cheese mixture among the tart shells. Cover with the figs and walnuts, divided equally among the shells. Bake the tartlets at 350°F, just to heat the filling through, about 5 minutes.

Yield: 4 first-course appetizers.

3
Meatless Entrées and Side Dishes

Spanakopita

Greek spinach pie continues to please taste buds, whether it's served at a picnic, on a buffet table, or as the entrée in a vegetarian meal.

2 (10-ounce) packages frozen chopped spinach, thawed and drained, or 2 cups chopped cooked spinach
1 cup thinly sliced green onions (including tops)
2 tablespoons olive oil
4 eggs, lightly beaten
8 ounces feta cheese, crumbled
1 cup small-curd cottage cheese
½ cup chopped parsley
2 tablespoons chopped fresh dill or 2 teaspoons dried dill weed
½ teaspoon salt
¼ teaspoon ground black pepper
¼ teaspoon ground nutmeg
¼ cup butter, melted, mixed with ¼ cup olive oil, for brushing filo
12 sheets filo

Squeeze the spinach dry; place it in a large bowl. In a small frying pan over medium heat, cook the green onions in the 2 tablespoons olive oil until limp. Add them to the spinach. Add the eggs, cheeses, parsley, dill, salt, pepper, and nutmeg; mix well.

Brush the bottom and sides of a 9 by 13-inch baking pan with the butter-oil mixture. Line the pan with six sheets of filo, brushing each sheet lightly with the butter-oil mixture and letting the filo overlap the sides of the pan. Spread the spinach mixture in the pan. Fold the overhanging filo over the filling.

Fold the remaining six sheets of filo to fit the pan; place them over the spinach, one at a time, brushing between layers with the butter-oil mixture. Brush the top with butter-oil mixture. If you are making the *spanakopita* ahead, cover and chill it up to 8 hours.

Preheat the oven to 375°F. Bake the *spanakopita*, uncovered, 40 to 45 minutes or until the filo is golden brown and a knife inserted in the center comes out clean. Cut the *spanakopita* into squares to serve. Serve it hot or at room temperature.

Yield: 12 servings

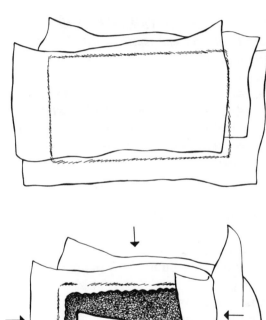

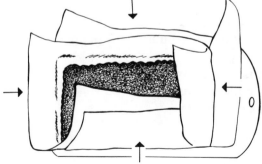

Borek

(see page 41)

My recipe card for Turkish cheese pie is yellowed with age and spattered with butter—a testament to its popularity in our family. The Stanford University student who taught me to make it explained that in her home country filo was brushed with a butter-milk mixture to make each filo layer extra crisp. You can double this recipe (bake it in a 9 x 13-inch pan) if you wish, but don't wait for a party to try what may become your standby for an easy family entrée.

8 ounces feta cheese
3 eggs
¼ cup chopped parsley
¼ teaspoon ground black pepper
Salt to taste
6 tablespoons butter
3 tablespoons milk
12 sheets filo

Crumble the cheese into a medium bowl. Add two of the eggs, one at a time, beating well after each addition. Beat the remaining egg in a small bowl. Pour half the egg into the cheese mixture; reserve the other half. Stir into the cheese mixture the parsley, pepper, and salt, if you wish (depending on the saltiness of the feta).

Melt the butter in a small pan; remove the pan from the heat, and stir in the milk.

Brush an 8-inch square pan with the butter-milk mixture. One sheet at a time, generously brush four sheets of filo with the butter-milk mixture, fold them in half lengthwise, and lay them in the pan, letting the filo overlap the sides of the pan as illustrated on page 41. Generously brush two sheets of filo with the butter-milk mixture and fold them to fit the pan. Place the folded sheets in the pan, and spread the cheese mixture over them. Top with four more sheets of filo brushed generously with the butter-milk mixture and folded to fit the pan. Fold in the overlapping edges. Fold the remaining two sheets of filo to fit the pan. Brush each generously with butter-milk mixture and place them in the pan. Brush the top with the reserved egg. If you are making the *borek* ahead, cover and chill it up to 4 hours.

Preheat the oven to 350°F. Bake the *borek*, uncovered, for 1 hour, or until the filo is puffed and golden brown and a knife inserted in the center comes out clean. Cut the *borek* into squares to serve. Serve it hot or at room temperature.

Yield: 6 servings

Artichoke-Mushroom Pie

The genie in the jar, marinated artichoke hearts, gives a piquant flavor to this family-pleasing entrée.

2 (6-ounce) jars marinated artichoke
    hearts
1 small onion, chopped
1 garlic clove, minced or pressed
¼ pound mushrooms, sliced
2 tablespoons chopped parsley
1 cup ricotta cheese
2 eggs
¼ cup grated Parmesan cheese
¼ teaspoon salt
¼ teaspoon ground black pepper
6 tablespoons butter, melted, for
    brushing filo
10 sheets filo

Drain the marinade from one jar of the artichokes into a wide frying pan. Drain the other jar, reserving the marinade for other uses. Chop all the artichokes, and set them aside.

Heat the marinade in the pan over medium heat, add the onion and garlic, and cook until the onion is limp. Add the mushrooms and cook, stirring occasionally, until the mushrooms are soft and the pan juices have evaporated. Stir in the parsley and artichoke hearts, and let the mixture cool.

Place the ricotta cheese in a large bowl. Beat in the eggs, one at a time. Stir in the Parmesan cheese, artichoke mixture, salt, and pepper.

Brush an 8-inch square pan with melted butter. One sheet at a time, lightly brush four sheets of filo with the butter and fold them in half lengthwise. Line the pan with them, letting them overlap the sides as illustrated on page 41. Brush two sheets of filo with butter and fold them to fit the pan. Place the folded sheets in the pan and spread the artichoke mixture over them. Top with two more sheets of filo brushed lightly with butter and folded to fit the pan. Fold in the overlapping edges. Fold the remaining two sheets of filo to fit the pan. Brush them lightly with butter, and place them in the pan. Brush the top of the pie with butter. If you are making the pie ahead, cover and chill it up to 4 hours.

Preheat the oven to 350°F. Bake the pie, uncovered, 35 to 40 minutes or until the filo is golden brown and a knife inserted in the center comes out clean. Cut the pie into squares to serve. Serve it hot or at room temperature.

Yield: 6 servings

Chèvre Pie

Think of this as a quiche, only easier. The filling is whipped up in minutes. Then all you need do is fold the filo to fit your pan. A crisp green salad would contrast nicely with the creamy filling.

1 garlic clove, cut in thirds
1 cup small-curd cottage cheese
3 eggs
½ cup all-purpose flour
½ cup milk
1 cup (4 ounces) shredded jack cheese
4 ounces goat cheese (chèvre), crumbled
2 tablespoons butter, melted and cooled
½ teaspoon dried thyme leaves
10 sheets filo
6 tablespoons butter, melted, for brushing filo

In a food processor, blend the garlic, cottage cheese, and eggs until smooth. Add the flour and milk; blend until the ingredients are evenly mixed. Add the jack cheese, goat cheese, 2 tablespoons melted butter, and thyme. Blend until the mixture is smooth.

Brush an 8-inch square pan with melted butter. One sheet at a time, lightly brush four sheets of filo with butter and fold them in half lengthwise. Line the pan with four sheets, letting them overlap the sides as illustrated on page 41. Lightly brush two sheets of filo with butter, and fold them to fit the pan. Place the folded sheets in the pan, and spread the cheese mixture over them. Top with two more sheets of filo brushed lightly with butter and folded to fit the pan. Fold in the overlapping edges. Fold the remaining two sheets of filo to fit the pan. Brush them lightly with butter, and place them in the pan. Brush the top of the pie with butter. If you are making the pie ahead, cover and chill it up to 4 hours.

Preheat the oven to 350°F. Bake the pie, uncovered, 35 to 40 minutes or until the filo is golden brown and a knife inserted in the center comes out clean. Cut the pie into squares to serve. Serve it hot or at room temperature.

Yield: 6 servings

French Onion Tart

❨❧❨❧❨❧❨❧❨❧❨❧❨❧❨❧❨❧❨❧❨❧❨❧❨❧❨

Cut this tart into small pieces to serve it as an appetizer, or serve large squares as a light entrée, accompanied by a crisp green salad.

3 tablespoons olive oil

3 large onions, cut in half lengthwise
    and thinly sliced lengthwise

¼ cup dry vermouth or dry white wine

½ teaspoon sugar

4 medium tomatoes, peeled, seeded,
    and chopped, or 1 (1-pound) can
    tomatoes, drained and chopped

1 tablespoon tomato paste

1 teaspoon dried basil

¼ teaspoon dried oregano

Salt and pepper to taste

8 sheets filo

5 tablespoons butter, melted, for
    brushing filo

¾ cup shredded Gruyère cheese

2 tablespoons sliced pitted ripe olives

2 tablespoons grated Parmesan cheese

Heat 2 tablespoons of the olive oil in a wide frying pan over medium-low heat. Add the onions, and stir to coat them with the oil. Cover the pan, and cook, stirring occasionally, for 10 minutes. Add the vermouth and sugar. Cook uncovered, stirring often, until the pan juices have evaporated and the onions are golden and glazed, about 20 more minutes. Let the mixture cool.

Heat the remaining 1 tablespoon oil in another frying pan over medium-high heat. Add the tomatoes, and cook for 5 minutes. Stir in the tomato paste, basil, and oregano. Cook until the mixture is thick, 6 to 8 minutes. Add the salt and pepper, and let the mixture cool.

Brush a 9-inch square pan with melted butter. Brush one sheet of filo lightly with melted butter, fold it in half lengthwise, and place it in the pan, letting the filo overlap opposite sides equally. Repeat with a second sheet of filo, but place it in the pan in the opposite direction so there is an over-hang on all four sides of the pan. Repeat with the remaining filo, laying it in alternating directions. Roll the overlapping sides to make a rim just inside the pan. Moisten the edges lightly with water to seal them. Brush the edges with butter.

Spread the onions over the filo. Top with the tomato mixture. Sprinkle with the Gruyère cheese and olives. Top with the Parmesan cheese. Bake the tart immediately, or cover and chill it up to 8 hours.

Preheat the oven to 350°F. Bake the tart, uncovered, 25 to 30 minutes or until the edges of the crust are golden brown. Serve the tart warm or at room temperature.

Yield: 9 servings

Filo Calzone

Unlike traditional calzone with its chewy pizza dough wrapper, filo calzone is crisp, flaky, and light. This shape takes more time to fold than a rectangular packet, but it's fun to make for special occasions and special guests.

1 pound Japanese eggplant or 1 small
　　standard eggplant, unpeeled, cut
　　lengthwise in ¼-inch thick slices
2 tablespoons olive oil
16 sheets filo
¼ cup oil from marinated sun-dried
　　tomatoes mixed with ¼ cup
　　additional olive oil, for brushing filo
½ cup sun-dried tomatoes marinated
　　in oil, drained and cut into strips
¼ teaspoon garlic powder
¼ cup sliced pitted ripe olives
1 cup (4 ounces) shredded mozzarella
　　cheese

Preheat the oven to 400° F. Place the eggplant in a single layer on a greased baking sheet. Brush with the 2 tablespoons olive oil. Bake the eggplant for 10 to 12 minutes, or until it is tender. Let it cool.

Stack four sheets of filo on your work surface, brushing each sheet lightly with the combined oils as you stack. Using the tip of a sharp knife and an 8-inch plate as a guide, cut out two circles. On half of each circle, place a slice of eggplant (cut to fit if necessary), a few tomato strips, a dash of garlic powder, a few olive slices, and 2 tablespoons of cheese. Leave a rim of about ¾ inch. Brush the entire rim of the circle with water. Fold the plain half over the filling. Fold over the rim, so the edge of the filo meets the filling, and press to seal. Place the calzone on an ungreased baking sheet and brush with oil. Repeat with the remaining ingredients. If you are making the calzones ahead, cover and chill them up to

8 hours.

Preheat the oven to 350°F. Bake the calzones, uncovered, 20 to 25 minutes or until the filo is golden brown. Serve them at once.

Yield: 8 servings

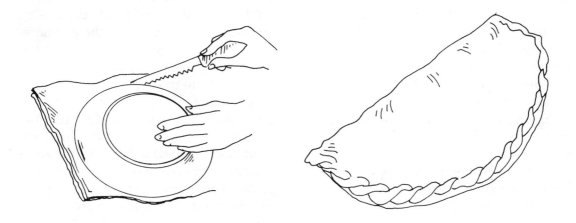

Swiss Chard and Cheese Squares

When you fold filo into a 4-inch square packet, you can stuff it with enough filling to transform it from a dainty tidbit to a satisfying entrée. This filling is dense, so each packet needs two sheets of filo.

1 medium onion, chopped
2 tablespoons olive oil
12 large leaves Swiss chard, coarsely chopped, or 2 (10-ounce) packages frozen Swiss chard, thawed and squeezed dry
3 cups sliced leeks (3 medium leeks), white part and about 2 inches of green leaves
1 large garlic clove, minced or pressed
¼ cup chopped parsley
½ teaspoon salt
¼ teaspoon ground black pepper
¼ teaspoon ground nutmeg
1 cup (4 ounces) shredded Swiss cheese

16 sheets filo
½ cup butter, melted, for brushing filo
2 tablespoons grated Parmesan cheese

In a 5-quart pan over medium heat, cook the onion in the oil until it is limp. Add the chard, leeks, and garlic, and cook, stirring occasionally, for 5 minutes. Cover the pan, and cook over low heat for 10 minutes or until the chard is tender. Add the parsley, and cook, uncovered, until the pan juices have evaporated. Stir in the salt, pepper, and nutmeg, and let the mixture cool. Stir the cheese into the cooled filling.

Lay a sheet of filo on your work surface, and brush it lightly with melted butter. Lay another sheet of filo over the first, and brush it with butter. Place ½ cup filling about 4 inches from one short edge of the filo, centered between the long sides. Spread the filling to make a 4-inch square. Fold the short edge of the filo over the filling. Fold the long sides over. Fold the filo completely to make a 4-inch square packet. Place the square seam side down in an ungreased baking pan. Brush it with butter, and sprinkle it with Parmesan cheese. Repeat this process to make seven more squares. Bake the squares immediately, or cover and chill them up to 8 hours.

Preheat the oven to 375°F. Bake the squares, uncovered, 20 to 25 minutes or until they are golden brown. Serve them hot.

Yield: 8 servings

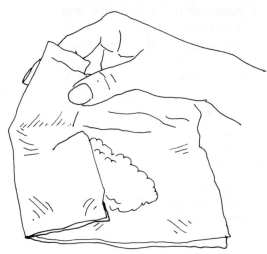

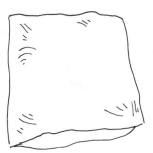

Chile-Potato Squares

1 pound thin-skinned potatoes
½ cup sour cream
½ cup small-curd cottage cheese
½ cup shredded Cheddar cheese
¼ cup canned diced green chiles
1 green onion (including top), thinly
   sliced
1 teaspoon mild ground red chili or
   chili powder
¼ teaspoon salt
12 sheets filo
6 tablespoons butter, melted, for
   brushing filo

In a pan, cook the potatoes in 2 inches of boiling water, covered, for 20 minutes, or until they are tender when pierced. Drain the potatoes, and let them cool. Peel the potatoes, and cut them into ¼-inch dice.

In a large bowl, combine the sour cream, the cheeses, the green chiles, the green onion, ½ teaspoon of the ground chili, and the salt. Stir in the potatoes.

Lay a sheet of filo on your work surface, and brush it lightly with melted butter. Lay another sheet of filo over the first, and brush it with butter. Place ½ cup of the filling about 4 inches from one short edge of the filo, centered between the long sides. Spread the filling to make a 4-inch square. Fold the short edge of the filo over the filling. Fold the long sides over. Fold the filo completely to make a 4-inch square packet as illustrated on page 53. Place the square seam side down in an ungreased baking pan. Brush with butter, and sprinkle with some of the remaining ground chili. Repeat this process to make five more squares. If you are making the squares ahead, cover and chill them up to 8 hours.

Preheat the oven to 375°F. Bake the squares, uncovered, 20 to 25 minutes or until the filo is golden brown. Serve them hot.

Yield: 6 servings

Anna's Romanian Soufflé

I've never met Anna Roder, but I'd like to peek in her kitchen and watch her in action. In her 84 years she has learned the secret of fine cooking: the simplest dish is often the best. Her recipe, shared by a friend, is not a classic soufflé, but a tender custard that bakes around puffy filo. It would be welcomed for brunch, lunch, or a light supper.

4 sheets filo
3 tablespoons butter, melted, for
  brushing filo
¾ cup shredded Gruyère or Swiss
  cheese
3 eggs
1 cup milk
½ teaspoon salt
⅛ teaspoon white pepper

Stack the filo horizontally on your work surface, brushing each sheet lightly with melted butter as you stack. Sprinkle the cheese over the bottom third of the filo. Roll up the filo very loosely, jelly-roll style. Coil the roll loosely in a greased 1-quart soufflé dish. Brush the coil with butter. If desired, cover and chill the dish up to 8 hours.

Preheat the oven to 350°F. In a bowl, beat the eggs lightly. Stir in the milk, salt, and pepper. Pour the mixture over the filo and into the center of the dish. Bake the soufflé, uncovered, for 30 to 35 minutes or until the top of the filo is golden, and a knife inserted in the center comes out clean. Serve the soufflé warm.

Yield: 4 servings

Filo Quesadillas

It's tempting to make up a recipe just to see how far one can go with filo, but taste is the final test. Our testers described this dish as simple and smashing.

½ cup shredded jack cheese
½ cup shredded Cheddar cheese
2 green onions (including tops), thinly
    sliced
¼ cup canned diced green chiles
1 tablespoon chopped cilantro
8 sheets filo
4 tablespoons butter, melted, for
    brushing filo

In a bowl, combine the cheeses, green onions, chiles, and cilantro. Stack four sheets of filo on your work surface, brushing each sheet lightly with melted butter as you stack. Using the tip of a sharp knife and an 8-inch plate as a guide, cut out two circles as illustrated on page 51. On half of each circle, place ¼ of the cheese mixture. Leave a rim of about ¾ inch. Brush the entire rim of the circle with water. Fold the plain half over the filling. Fold over the rim, so the edge of the filo meets the filling, and press to seal. Place the quesadilla on an ungreased baking sheet and brush with butter. Repeat with the remaining ingredients. If you are making the quesadillas ahead, cover and chill them up to 8 hours.

Preheat the oven to 350° F. Bake the quesadillas, uncovered, 20 to 25 minutes or until the filo is golden brown. Serve them at once.

Yield: 4 servings

Gingered Carrot and Jicama Rolls

1 small onion, chopped
2 tablespoons butter
2 cups shredded carrots
2 tablespoons water
1 ½ teaspoons sugar
½ teaspoon lemon juice
¼ teaspoon salt
¼ teaspoon ground ginger
⅛ teaspoon ground black pepper
1 cup shredded jicama
¼ cup sour cream
12 sheets filo
6 tablespoons butter, melted, for
    brushing filo

In a wide frying pan over medium heat, cook the onion in the 2 tablespoons butter until limp. Add the carrots, water, sugar, lemon juice, salt, ginger, and pepper. Cover the pan, and cook over low heat for 5 minutes. Squeeze the jicama dry, add it to the pan, and cook the mixture, covered, for 5 more minutes or until the carrots are barely tender. Uncover the pan, and cook briefly until the pan juices have evaporated. Let the mixture cool, then stir in the sour cream.

Lay a sheet of filo horizontally on your work surface, and brush it lightly with melted butter. Lay another sheet of filo over the first, and brush it with butter. Cut the filo in half crosswise. For each roll, spread about ⅓ cup filling in a band along the bottom 2 inches from the edge; leave a 2-inch margin at either side. Fold the bottom edge over the filling. Fold in the sides. Roll up the filo jelly-roll style. Place the roll seam side down in an ungreased baking pan. Brush with butter. Repeat this process with the remaining ingredients. You can cover and chill them up to 8 hours.

Preheat the oven to 350°F. Bake the rolls, uncovered, for 20 to 25 minutes or until they are golden brown.

Yield: 12 servings

Spring Rolls

Here is a different slant on a Chinese spring roll baked painlessly in the oven.

4 dried black mushrooms
1 tablespoon vegetable oil
2 garlic cloves, minced
1 teaspoon minced fresh ginger
1 cup carrot cut in fine julienne strips
3 cups finely shredded cabbage
1 cup jicama cut in fine julienne strips
3 greens onions (including tops), cut in
   1-inch shreds
¼ cup chicken broth or water
4 ounces tofu, drained and crumbled
2 tablespoons soy sauce
1 teaspoon sugar
¼ teaspoon each salt and pepper
2 teaspoons sesame oil
2 teaspoons cornstarch mixed with 1
   tablespoon water
10 sheets filo
5 tablespoons butter, melted, mixed
with 1 teaspoon sesame oil, for
   brushing filo
Sesame seeds for topping

Soak the mushrooms in warm water to cover for 30 minutes; drain them. Cut off and discard the stems; thinly slice the caps.

Heat the oil in a wok or wide frying pan over high heat. When the oil is hot, add the garlic and ginger, and cook for 5 seconds. Add the carrot, and stir-fry it for 30 seconds. Add the mushrooms, cabbage, jicama, green onions, and broth or water. Stir to combine the vegetables. Cover and steam for 2 minutes, or until the vegetables are barely tender. Add the tofu, soy sauce, sugar, salt, pepper, and sesame oil. Add the cornstarch solution and cook, stirring, until the pan juices thicken slightly. If the mixture is very juicy, thicken it with a little more cornstarch solution. Remove the pan from the heat, and let the mixture cool.

Lay a sheet of filo horizontally on your work surface, and brush it lightly with the butter-oil mixture. Lay another sheet of filo over the first, and brush it with the butter-oil mixture. Cut the filo in half crosswise as illustrated on page 85. For each roll, spread ¼ cup filling in a band along the bottom, 2 inches from the edge; leave a 2-inch margin at either side. Fold the bottom edge over the filling. Fold in the sides. Fold the filo completely to make a packet about 6 inches by 2 inches. Place the packet seam side down in an ungreased baking pan. Brush it with butter. Sprinkle a few sesame seeds over the top. Repeat this process with the remaining ingredients. If you are making the spring rolls ahead, cover and chill them up to 4 hours.

Preheat the oven to 375°F. Bake the spring rolls, uncovered, 20 to 25 minutes, or until they are golden brown. Serve them hot.

Yield: 10 servings

Cheese Blintzes with Cherry Sauce

Traditional blintzes are made with thin pan-cakes wrapped around a filling of cottage cheese or fruit and pan-fried. To make your enter-taining more leisurely, replace the crêpes with filo, then pop a panful in the oven when the guests arrive.

2 cups (1 pound) farmer cheese
2 egg yolks
2 tablespoons sugar
1 teaspoon lemon juice
½ teaspoon vanilla
16 sheets filo
⅔ cup butter, melted, for brushing filo

Sweet Cherry Sauce
¼ cup sugar
2 teaspoons cornstarch
½ cup water
2 teaspoons lemon juice
2 cups pitted fresh or frozen, thawed
  bing cherries

In a food processor or electric mixer, blend the cheese, egg yolks, sugar, lemon juice, and vanilla until smooth. Lay a sheet of filo horizontally on your work surface, and brush it lightly with melted butter. Lay another sheet of filo over the first, and brush it with butter. Cut the filo in half crosswise as illustrated on page 85. For each blintz, spread 2 tablespoons filling in a band along the bottom edge 2 inches from the bottom; leave a 2-inch margin at either side. Fold the bottom edge over the filling. Fold in the sides. Fold the filo completely to make a packet about 6 inches by 2 inches. Place the packet seam side down in an ungreased baking pan. Brush it with butter. Repeat this process with the remaining ingredients. If you are making the blintzes ahead, cover and chill them up to 24 hours.

To make the sauce, in a 2-quart pan stir together the sugar, cornstarch, water, and lemon juice until smooth. Add the cherries.

Cook over medium heat, stirring, until the sauce has thickened slightly.

Preheat the oven to 350°F. Bake the blintzes, uncovered, 20 to 25 minutes or until they are golden brown. Serve them hot, topped with warm cherry sauce.

Yield: 8 servings (16 blintzes)

Potato-Onion Blintzes

Sautéed onion enlivens these mildly seasoned packets.

2 medium onions, finely chopped
2 tablespoons butter
2 cups mashed, unseasoned potatoes
   (3 medium potatoes)
1 egg, lightly beaten
½ teaspoon salt
¼ teaspoon pepper
16 sheets filo
⅔ cup butter, melted, for brushing filo
Sour cream or plain yogurt and sliced
   chives for topping

In a wide frying pan over medium heat, cook the onions in the 2 tablespoons butter for 15 minutes or until they are very soft. Let the onions cool. In a bowl, combine the potatoes, onions, egg, salt, and pepper; mix well.

Lay a sheet of filo horizontally on your work surface, and brush it lightly with the melted butter. Lay another sheet of filo over the first, and brush it with butter. Cut the filo in half crosswise as illustrated on page 85. For each blintz, spread 2 table-spoons filling in a band along the bottom edge, 2 inches from the bottom; leave a 2-inch margin at either side. Fold the bottom edge over the filling. Fold in the sides. Fold the filo completely to make a packet about 2 inches by 6 inches. Place the packet seam side down in an ungreased baking pan. Brush it with butter. Repeat this process with the remaining ingredients. If you are making the blintzes ahead, cover and chill them up to 24 hours.

Preheat the oven to 350°F. Bake the blintzes, uncovered, 20 to 25 minutes or until they are lightly browned. Serve them hot topped with sour cream and chives.

Yield: 8 servings (16 blintzes)

4
Poultry, Seafood, and Meat Entrées

Filo Poultry Packets

One hour of preparation will provide a fine hurry-up weekday meal when you wrap and freeze poultry packets. The poultry is not cooked first so the wrapping goes quickly. Then, on a night when you are rushed and tired and have no interest in cooking—or when you suddenly decide to invite guests— pull this convenience food from your freezer and let the oven do the work.

For each packet, you need two sheets of filo, a seasoning mixture (suggestions follow), and one 5- to 6-ounce boneless, skinless chicken breast half or 5 to 6 ounces of turkey breast slices (also called turkey cutlets). Turkey breast slices are cut ¼ inch thick and weigh from 2 to 3 ounces each. For each packet, stack two slices, and treat them as one piece. If you bone turkey breast yourself, cut the slices ½ inch thick. Before wrapping, press the poultry dry between paper towels.

To wrap each packet, lay one sheet of filo on your work surface, and brush it lightly with melted butter or oil (about 2 teaspoons). Lay another sheet over the first, and brush it with butter. Spread the seasoning mixture on one side of the poultry. Place the poultry, seasoned side down, about 2 inches from a short side of the filo, centered between the long sides. Top the poultry with additional seasoning mixture. Flip the end of the filo over the poultry and fold once; then fold both long sides of the filo over the poultry, and fold up the packet completely to make a rectangle about 3 by 5 inches.

Place the packet, seam side down, on an ungreased baking sheet, brush it with butter or oil, and sprinkle with the topping, if you are using one. If you are going to bake the packets within 24 hours, cover and chill them. For longer storage, freeze them solid on the baking sheet, then transfer them to a container with a tight-fitting lid and return them to the freezer. Bake packets, uncovered, in a preheated 375°F. oven for 25 minutes (30 minutes if frozen) or until the filo is golden brown.

Each of the following six recipes—easily doubled or tripled for a party—suggest a type of poultry to use, but feel free to substitute one for the other. By nature, turkey breast is not as tender as chicken breast. It tastes best when complemented with zesty seasonings.

3

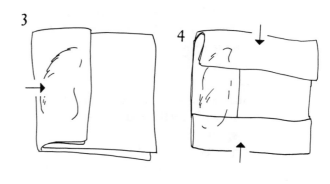

4

5

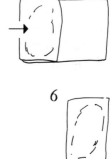

6

1

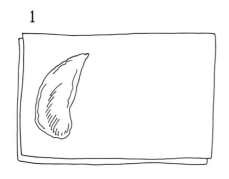

2

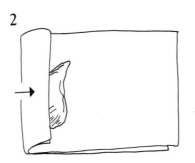

Chicken with Herb Cheese

Widely available, creamy cheese spreads come in several flavors. You may want to try one with garlic and spices, instead of herbs, or a French onion spread.

1 (4-ounce) package creamy cheese
    spread with garlic and herbs
1 tablespoon chopped parsley
½ teaspoon dried basil
Ground black pepper to taste
5 boneless, skinless chicken breast
    halves
10 sheets filo
7 tablespoons butter, melted, mixed
    with 1 pressed garlic clove, for
    brushing filo

In a bowl, blend together the cheese spread, parsley, basil, and pepper. Use about 1 tablespoon of the mixture to coat each side of the chicken breast halves. Assemble and bake the packets as explained on page 64, brushing the filo with garlic butter.

Yield: 5 servings

Poulet Dijonnaise

This calls for Dijon mustard and a coarse-grain mustard, but you may use any mustard that appeals to you. Look for black mustard seeds in a gourmet store or an Indian market. They are not as biting hot as regular mustard seeds.

⅓ cup sour cream
3 tablespoons Dijon mustard
3 tablespoons coarse-grain mustard
1 teaspoon Italian herb seasoning
6 boneless, skinless chicken breast
   halves
12 sheets filo
½ cup butter, melted, for brushing filo
Black mustard seeds for topping

In a bowl, whisk together the sour cream, mustards, and herb seasoning until smooth. Use about 1 tablespoon to coat each side of the chicken breast halves. Assemble and bake the packets as explained on page 64. After buttering the tops of the packets, sprinkle them with a few mustard seeds.

Yield: 6 servings

Jalapeño Chicken

Taste the seasoned mayonnaise before brushing it on the chicken. If you like food really hot, you may want to add more chile. This is nice topped with sour cream and a zingy salsa.

¾ cup mayonnaise
1 ½ tablespoons lemon juice
3 tablespoons chopped cilantro
1 ½ to 2 teaspoons minced, seeded
   jalapeño or *serrano* chile
6 boneless, skinless chicken breast
   halves
12 sheets filo
½ cup butter, melted, for brushing filo

In a bowl, combine the mayonnaise, lemon juice, cilantro, and chile. Use about 1 tablespoon of the mixture to coat each side of the chicken breast halves. Assemble and bake the packets as explained on page 64.

Yield: 6 servings

Chicken with Mushroom Pâté

Sweet and creamy, mushroom pâté soothes rather than teases your taste buds.

1 small onion, finely chopped
2 tablespoons butter
½ pound mushrooms, finely chopped
2 tablespoons chopped parsley
2 tablespoons dry white wine
¼ teaspoon dried thyme leaves
¼ cup sour cream
¼ cup mayonnaise
Salt and pepper to taste
6 boneless, skinless chicken breast
　　halves
12 sheets filo
½ cup butter, melted, for brushing filo
Grated Parmesan cheese for topping

In a wide frying pan over medium heat, cook the onion in the 2 tablespoons butter until limp. Add the mushrooms, parsley, wine, and thyme. Increase the heat to medium-high. Cook the mixture 6 to 8 minutes, or until it is lightly browned and the pan juices have evaporated. Let the mixture cool. Stir in the sour cream, mayonnaise, and salt and pepper. Use about 1 tablespoon of the mixture to coat each side of the chicken breast halves. Assemble and bake the packets as explained on page 64. After buttering the tops of the packets, sprinkle them with Parmesan cheese.

Yield: 6 servings

Turkey Milanese

Italian cooks sprinkle this zesty seasoning, called gremolata, *over veal shanks. It gives an exciting flavor punch to turkey, too.*

¾ cup chopped parsley
1 tablespoon grated lemon zest
2 teaspoons grated orange zest
1 large garlic clove, minced or pressed
3 tablespoons olive oil
12 (3-ounce) turkey breast slices,
   cut ¼ -inch-thick
Salt to taste
12 sheets filo
6 tablespoons butter, melted, mixed
   with 2 tablespoons olive oil, for
   brushing filo
Grated Parmesan cheese for topping

In a bowl, combine the parsley, lemon and orange zests, garlic, and the 3 tablespoons olive oil. For each packet, stack two turkey slices together, and sprinkle them lightly with salt. Spread about 1 tablespoon of the parsley mixture on each side of the turkey stack. Assemble and bake the packets as directed on page 64, brushing the tops of the packets with the butter-oil mixture and sprinkling with Parmesan cheese.

Yield: 6 servings

Turkey Saltimbocca

This packet holds an intriguing contrast of textures: tender turkey, creamy cheese, and chewy prosciutto all wrapped in crispy filo.

12 (3-ounce) turkey breast slices, cut
  ¼-inch-thick
12 fresh sage leaves or ½ teaspoon
  dried rubbed sage
6 ounces fontina or jack cheese, cut
  into 6 thin slices
6 very thin slices prosciutto (about 3
  ounces)
12 sheets filo
¼ cup butter, melted, mixed with ¼
  cup olive oil, for brushing filo

For each packet, stack two turkey slices together, and top them with two sage leaves or sprinkle them with dried sage. Top with a slice of cheese then wrap the turkey and cheese with a slice of prosciutto. Assemble and bake the packets as directed on page 64, brushing the filo with the butter–olive oil mixture.

Yield: 6 servings

Old-Fashioned Chicken Pot Pies

Unlike most frozen pot pies which contain more gravy than chicken, these are chock-full of tender chicken nuggets and garden-sweet vegetables, bound together in a silky sauce.

Chicken
1 frying chicken (3 to 4 pounds), cut up
1 medium onion, coarsely chopped
1 small carrot, sliced
1 stalk celery, sliced
3 sprigs parsley
1 bay leaf
¼ teaspoon whole black peppercorns

2 medium carrots, diced
1 small turnip, diced
10 small white boiling onions, peeled
¼ pound small whole mushrooms
½ cup frozen peas, thawed
3 tablespoons butter
3 tablespoons all-purpose flour

⅔ cup light cream
½ teaspoon salt
¼ teaspoon ground black pepper
¼ teaspoon ground nutmeg
2 tablespoons chopped parsley
8 to 12 sheets filo
4 to 6 tablespoons butter, melted, for brushing filo

To prepare the chicken, set the breast pieces aside. Place the remaining chicken pieces in a 5-quart pan with the onion, carrot, celery, parsley, bay leaf, and black peppercorns. Barely cover the contents with water. Bring to a boil, cover the pan, and simmer the ingredients for 20 minutes. Add the breast pieces. Continue to cook for 35 to 40 minutes or until the chicken is tender. Lift out the chicken pieces, and let them cool. Remove the skin and bones; cut the meat into bite-size pieces, and set them aside.

Strain the broth; discard the seasonings.

Skim all the fat from the broth. Bring the broth to a boil, and add the diced carrots and turnip, onions, and the mushrooms. Simmer them for 10 minutes. Add the peas, and cook 2 minutes more. With a slotted spoon, scoop out the vegetables and set them aside. Measure 1 ⅓ cups broth, and reserve it.

Melt the 3 tablespoons butter in a 2-quart pan over medium heat. Add the flour and cook, stirring, until the mixture is golden. Whisk in the reserved broth and the cream. Cook, stirring, until the sauce is smooth and thick. Remove it from the heat and whisk in the salt, pepper, and nutmeg. Let the sauce cool, then fold in the parsley, chicken, and vegetables. Divide the mixture among six ramekins, about 1 ½-cup size.

Stack eight sheets of filo on your work surface, brushing each sheet lightly with melted butter as you stack. Using the tip of a sharp knife and a plate as your guide, cut out six circles of filo, each 2 inches larger than the diameter of the ramekins. If you haven't enough filo to make six circles, fold four more sheets in half crosswise to make eight layers. Brush one half of each sheet with butter before folding over the other half, then brush the top. Stack the folded sheets together, and cut out as many circles as needed. Place the filo rounds over the chicken mixture in the ramekins. Roll the edges down toward the centers so the crusts fit snugly in the ramekins. Cut slits in the tops, and brush with butter. If you are making the pies ahead, cover and chill them up to 24 hours.

Preheat the oven to 375°F. Bake the pies, uncovered, 30 to 40 minutes or until the chicken is bubbly and the filo is golden brown. Serve them hot.

Yield: 6 servings

Bisteeya

If you're looking for something as exotic as The Arabian Nights, *you'll find this lavish Moroccan specialty utterly delicious and intriguing to make.*

1 frying chicken (3 to 4 pounds), cut
   up
1 medium onion, chopped
¾ cup chopped parsley
¼ cup chopped cilantro
3 cups chicken broth or 1 can (14 ½
   ounces) chicken broth and 1
   cup water
1 3-inch cinnamon stick
½ teaspoon ground ginger
½ teaspoon saffron threads
¼ teaspoon ground black pepper
1 cup blanched almonds, finely
   chopped
2 tablespoons granulated sugar
½ teaspoon ground cinnamon
6 eggs

¼ cup butter, melted, for brushing filo
8 sheets filo
Powdered sugar and ground cinnamon
   for garnish

Place the chicken, including the neck and giblets (save the liver for another use), in a 5-quart kettle. Add the onion, parsley, cilantro, chicken broth, cinnamon stick, ginger, saffron, and pepper. Bring to a boil. Reduce the heat, cover the pan, and simmer the ingredients 1 hour, or until the chicken pulls easily from the bones.

While the chicken cooks, toast the nuts in a 300°F. oven for 10 minutes, or until they are lightly browned; let them cool. In a bowl, combine the nuts, sugar, and cinnamon.

Lift the chicken and giblets from the broth with a slotted spoon. Let them stand until they are cool enough to handle. Then discard the skin and bones, and shred the meat into bite-size pieces. Chop the giblets.

Bring the unstrained broth to a boil over medium heat. In a bowl, lightly beat the eggs. Slowly pour the eggs into the broth, stirring until they form soft curds, 1 to 2 minutes. Pour the broth through a wire strainer placed over a bowl. Leave the strainer in place until the eggs are very well drained. Discard the cinnamon stick.

Lightly brush the bottom and sides of a 10-inch pie pan with the melted butter. One sheet at a time, lightly brush six sheets of filo with butter, and lay them in the pan. Overlap them on the bottom of the pan and let them extend 5 or 6 inches beyond the edges. Place the chicken in an even layer over the filo. Spread the eggs over the chicken, and sprinkle the almonds over the eggs. Fold the edges of the filo over the filling. Brush the filo with butter. Fold the remaining two sheets of filo in half crosswise, and place them on the pie. Tuck their edges inside the pan. Brush the top with butter. If you are making the pie ahead, cover and chill it up to 4 hours.

Preheat the oven to 425°F. Bake the pie, uncovered, for 20 to 25 minutes or until it is golden brown. Hold an unrimmed baking sheet loosely over the top of the pie; invert the pie pan and lift it off. Place the baking sheet in the oven, and bake the pie for 10 more minutes, or until the filo is golden brown. Invert the pie onto a platter, and let it stand for 5 minutes. Sift powdered sugar generously over the top. Holding pinches of cinnamon between your thumb and forefinger, decorate the pie with a grid of cinnamon lines, about 1 ½ inches apart. Cut the pie into wedges, and serve it hot.

Yield: 8 servings

Salmon with Balsamic Butter Sauce

For those of us unlucky enough to live too far from his restaurant in Ithaca, New York, Abby Nash shares his recipe for making a salmon spectacular at home. Describing it as assertive in flavor and good with red wine, he suggests one of the California Rhone-style blends or a young pinot noir. For a simpler preparation, omit the sauce.

6 sun-dried tomatoes marinated in oil, drained and minced
2 medium shallots, minced
4 teaspoons capers, rinsed and minced
1 tablespoon minced fresh basil or Italian parsley
1 garlic clove, minced or pressed
4 (6-ounce) boned and skinned salmon fillets
Salt and pepper to taste
10 sheets filo
6 tablespoons unsalted butter, melted, for brushing filo

Balsamic Butter Sauce
2 medium shallots, minced
3 tablespoons balsamic vinegar
3 tablespoons dry red wine such as zinfandel or petite sirah
2 tablespoons heavy cream
1 cup cold unsalted butter, cut into 16 pieces
1 teaspoon lemon juice
2 or 3 drops hot pepper sauce
Salt and pepper to taste

For the stuffing, combine the sun-dried tomatoes, shallots, capers, basil or parsley, and garlic in a bowl; set the bowl aside.

Butterfly the salmon fillets: split them horizontally almost all the way through, leaving one long edge attached. Spread open the two halves, and spread each with ¼ of the stuffing. Fold the halves together again to cover the stuffing.

Stack five sheets of filo horizontally on

your work surface, brushing each sheet lightly with melted butter as you stack. Cut the stack in half crosswise. Trim each half to make a square of about 9 inches. For each packet, sprinkle a salmon fillet with salt and pepper. Place the fillet in the center of the square. Fold the filo over the fish on all sides, brushing with butter after each fold. Place the packet seam side down in an ungreased baking pan, and brush the top with butter. Repeat this process with the remaining ingredients. If you are making the packets ahead, cover and chill them up to 4 hours.

Preheat the oven to 350°F. Bake the packets, uncovered, in the lower third of the oven for 10 minutes. Remove the packets from the oven and preheat the broiler. Watching very closely, broil the packets 4 or 5 inches from the heat until the top of the filo is golden brown, about 45 seconds.

While the salmon bakes, prepare the sauce. In a small pan over medium heat, cook the shallots, vinegar, and wine until the liquid is reduced to 2 teaspoons. Watch carefully, as it can burn easily. Add the cream, and cook until the liquid is reduced by one-half. Over low heat, add the butter, one piece at a time. Whisking constantly, add more butter just before the previous piece has emulsified. Add the lemon juice and hot sauce. Taste; add salt and pepper. Strain the sauce over the salmon packets.

Yield: 4 servings

Swordfish Teriyaki

I never learned origami when we lived in Japan, but I learned to tie food with kampyo *for esthetic appeal. The strips of dried gourd, available in Japanese markets, look like long shoelaces. You simmer them in broth to infuse them with flavor; their texture is pleasantly chewy. If you feel too many strings are tied to this recipe, omit this optional step. If you decide to go all the way, cook* kampyo *and freeze it in small portions for emergency ties.*

Kampyo
½ (3-ounce) package *kampyo* (dried gourd strips)
¼ cup chicken broth
2 tablespoons soy sauce
1 tablespoon dry sherry
2 teaspoons sugar

Teriyaki Sauce
¼ cup orange juice
3 tablespoons soy sauce
2 tablespoons dry sherry
1 tablespoon honey
2 quarter-size slices fresh ginger, crushed
Dash cayenne pepper

4 (4- or 5-ounce) boneless, skinless ¾-inch thick swordfish steaks
4 dried black mushrooms
2 green onions, cut into 1-inch slivers
1 (1-inch) slice fresh ginger, peeled and slivered
8 sheets filo
¼ cup butter, melted, mixed with 2 teaspoons sesame oil, for brushing filo

Wet the *kampyo* with water. Sprinkle it lightly with salt, and rub it together briefly with your hands. Rinse off the salt. Parboil the *kampyo* in water to cover for 10 minutes. Drain it. In a pan, combine the chicken broth, soy, sherry, and sugar. Add the *kampyo*, and stir to coat it with the liquid. Cook the *kampyo* over low heat, partially covered, until most of the pan juices have evaporated. Let it cool. Chill it until you are ready to use it.

For the sauce, in a glass baking dish combine the orange juice, soy, sherry, honey, ginger, and cayenne. Add the fish and turn it to coat it with the liquid. Cover and chill the fish for 1 hour, turning it several times in the marinade. Meanwhile soak the mushrooms in warm water to cover them for 30 minutes; drain them. Cut off and discard the stems; thinly slice the caps.

Lift the fish from the marinade, and pat it dry with paper towels. Lay a sheet of filo on your work surface, and brush it lightly with the butter–sesame oil mixture. Lay another sheet of filo on top of the first, and brush it with the butter-oil mixture. Place the fish on the filo, centered between the long sides, about 2 inches from one short end. Top the fish with a quarter of the dried mushrooms, green onions, and slivered ginger. Fold the end of the filo over the fish. Fold in the long sides, then fold the packet completely so it is seam side down. Cut a long piece of *kampyo*, and tie it in a knot around the middle of packet. Do not tie it in a bow but leave a 1-inch extension beyond the knot. Place the packet in an ungreased baking pan, and brush it with the butter-oil mixture. Repeat this process with the remaining ingredients. If you are making the packets ahead, cover and chill them up to 4 hours.

Preheat the oven to 400°F. Bake the packets, uncovered, for 15 to 18 minutes or until they are golden brown.

Yield: 4 servings

Filo-wrapped Halibut with Thai Pesto

Cilantro, chile, and garlic are made into a mildly hot pesto with peanuts to season, but not upstage, the halibut. The fish I buy comes in large pieces with neither bones nor skin. If you buy halibut steaks from a smaller fish, be sure to remove all the bones before wrapping in filo.

Thai Pesto

2 cups packed cilantro, heavy stems removed
2 garlic cloves, peeled
1 to 2 teaspoons sliced seeded *jalapeño* or *serrano* chile
¼ cup roasted peanuts
¼ cup vegetable oil
Salt to taste

4 (4- or 5-ounce) boneless, skinless ¾-inch-thick halibut pieces
8 sheets filo
5 tablespoons butter, melted, for brushing filo

In a food processor, finely chop the cilantro, garlic, chile, and peanuts. Add the oil, and blend to make a rough paste. Add salt.

Lay a sheet of filo on your work surface, and brush it lightly with the melted butter. Lay another sheet of filo on top of the first, and brush it with butter. Spread about 1 tablespoon pesto on each side of a piece of fish. Place the fish about 2 inches from one short end of the filo, centered between the long sides. Fold the end of the filo over the fish. Fold in the long sides, then fold the packet completely. Place the packet, seam side down, in an ungreased baking pan and brush it with butter. Repeat this process with the remaining ingredients. You can cover and chill the packets up to 4 hours.

Preheat the oven to 400°F. Bake the packets, uncovered, for 15 to 18 minutes, or until they are golden brown.

Yield: 4 servings

Pecan-Coated Fish Sticks

For this easy baked fish coated with filo flakes you can use any firm fish fillets, as long as they are 3/4 inch thick.

¼ cup vegetable oil
1 garlic clove, peeled and crushed
¼ teaspoon salt
1 ½ cups filo flakes
½ cup finely chopped pecans
Salt to taste
1 ½ pounds ¾-inch-thick fillets of
   white fish (snapper, turbot,
   cod, or sea bass)

In a wide shallow bowl, combine the oil, garlic, and salt. Let stand for 15 minutes.

In another bowl, combine the filo flakes and pecans; add a dash of salt if the nuts are not salted.

Remove any skin and bones from the fish. Cut the fillets crosswise into 1½-inch wide pieces. Dip each piece of fish in the seasoned oil, then coat it on both sides with the nut mixture. Arrange the fish in a single layer, without crowding, in a lightly greased baking pan. Preheat the oven to 450°F. Bake the fish for 8 to 12 minutes, or until it flakes when probed with a fork in the thickest part.

Yield: 4 or 5 servings

Filo Flakes

When you have filo trimmings, don't throw them away. Spread them in an ungreased baking pan, sprinkle them with water or melted butter, and bake them in a 350°F. oven for 10 minutes, or until they are golden brown. When they are cool, crush them into flakes with your hands and store them in an airtight container. Use in the same manner as dry bread crumbs.

Crab Rolls

Prescription for the TV snack food blahs: a hot crab sandwich wrapped in buttery filo and a glass of ice cold beer.

½ cup mayonnaise
1 teaspoon Dijon mustard
½ teaspoon dried tarragon
⅔ pound cooked crab meat, flaked
½ cup shredded Swiss cheese
⅓ cup finely chopped celery
¼ cup chopped green bell pepper
2 green onions (including tops), thinly
  sliced
8 sheets filo
5 tablespoons butter, melted, for
  brushing filo

In a bowl, whisk together the mayonnaise, mustard, and tarragon until smooth. Add the crab meat, cheese, celery, bell pepper, and green onions; mix well.

Lay a sheet of filo horizontally on your work surface, and brush it lightly with melted butter. Lay another sheet of filo on top of the first, and brush it with butter. Cut the filo in half crosswise. For each roll, spread about ⅓ cup filling in a band along the bottom edge of the filo, 2 inches from the edge; leave a 2-inch margin at either side. Fold the bottom edge over the filling. Fold in the sides. Roll up the filo jelly-roll style. Place the roll seam side down in an ungreased baking pan. Brush the top with butter. Repeat this process with the remaining ingredients. If you are making the rolls ahead, cover and chill them up to 8 hours.

Preheat the oven to 350°F. Bake the rolls, uncovered, 20 to 25 minutes or until the edges of the filo are golden brown.

Yield: 8 servings

Left Bank Pastelles

Michele Dumesnil, a French cooking teacher, remembers when filo became popular in France. "Dozens of small Tunisian and Algerian restaurants opened in Paris after World War II, and they sold wonderful, inexpensive food, much of it wrapped in filo." In Tunisia, pastelles are deep-fried and called brik. *Michele Dumesnil's baked version looks like a crispy tuna turnover.*

1 (6 ½-ounce) can solid white tuna, flaked
3 hard-boiled eggs, coarsely chopped
1 small onion, finely chopped
¼ cup chopped parsley
1 tablespoon lemon juice
¼ teaspoon ground black pepper
12 sheets filo
6 tablespoons butter, melted, for brushing filo
Lemon wedges

Combine the tuna, eggs, onion, parsley, lemon juice, and pepper in a bowl. Stack four sheets of filo on your work surface, brushing each sheet lightly with melted butter as you stack. Using the tip of a sharp knife and an 8-inch plate as a guide, cut out two circles (page 51). On half of each circle, place ⅙ of the tuna mixture. Leave a rim of about ¾. Brush the entire rim of the circle with water. Fold the plain half over the filling. Fold over the rim, so the edge of the filo meets the filling, and press to seal the edges. Place the pastelle in an ungreased baking pan, and brush it with butter. Repeat this process with the remaining ingredients. You can chill these up to 8 hours.

Preheat the oven to 350°F. Bake the pastelles, uncovered, 20 to 25 minutes, or until they are golden brown. Serve them hot with wedges of lemon to squeeze over.

Yield: 6 servings

Stroganoff Strudels

For a Russian repast, accompany these savory rolls with crisp cole slaw and tiny pickled beets.

1 medium onion, chopped
1 garlic clove, minced or pressed
1 tablespoon vegetable oil
1 pound ground chuck
¼ pound mushrooms, thinly sliced
¾ cup dry red wine
1 tablespoon tomato paste
1 teaspoon dried dill weed
¾ teaspoon salt
½ teaspoon ground black pepper
2 tablespoons chopped parsley
2 teaspoons prepared horseradish
½ cup sour cream
9 sheets filo
5 tablespoons butter, melted, for
　　brushing filo
¼ cup dry bread crumbs

In a wide frying pan over medium heat, cook the onion and garlic in the oil until the onion is limp. Crumble in the beef; cook until it is lightly browned. Add the mushrooms, and cook, stirring occasionally, until the mushrooms are soft. Drain off and discard the drippings.

In a bowl, whisk together the wine, tomato paste, dill weed, salt, and pepper. Stir this into the meat mixture. Cover the pan, and simmer for 10 minutes, or until the meat absorbs the sauce. Remove the pan from the heat, and stir in the parsley, horseradish, and sour cream. Let the mixture cool.

Lay a sheet of filo horizontally on your work surface, and brush it lightly with melted butter. Sprinkle with 1/2 teaspoon crumbs. Cover with a second sheet of filo. Brush it with butter, and sprinkle it with crumbs. Cover with a third sheet, and brush it with butter. Cut the filo in half crosswise. Spread

1/2 cup of the meat mixture in a band along one edge of the filo, 2 inches from the edge; leave a 2 inch margin at either side. Fold the bottom edge over the filling. Fold in the sides. Fold the filo completely to make a packet about 6 by 2 inches. Place the packet seam side down in an ungreased baking pan, and brush it with butter. Repeat this process with the remaining ingredients.

If you are making the strudels ahead, cover and chill them up to 24 hours. Preheat the oven to 375°F. Bake the strudels, uncovered, 20 to 25 minutes or until they are golden brown.

Yield: 6 servings

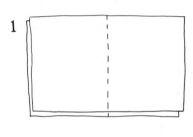

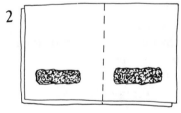

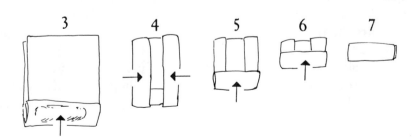

Jambalaya Rolls

You can play around with this recipe by using different kinds of sausage. If you buy uncooked sausage, perhaps a specialty of your local sausage maker, cook it through before adding the rice.

1 small onion, chopped
½ cup sliced celery
½ cup chopped red or green bell pepper
2 tablespoons butter
½ cup thinly sliced green onions (including tops)
6 ounces fully cooked spicy smoked cooked sausage (such as kielbasa), diced
½ teaspoon turmeric
3 cups cooked long-grain white rice (1 cup uncooked)
¼ cup chicken broth
½ teaspoon salt
¼ teaspoon ground black pepper
1 ½ cups diced cooked chicken

½ cup raisins, plumped in hot water and drained
12 sheets filo
½ cup butter, melted, for brushing filo

In a 5-quart pan over medium heat, cook the onion, celery, and bell pepper in the 2 tablespoons butter until the onion is limp. Add the green onions, sausage, and turmeric and cook for 2 minutes. Add the rice, chicken broth, salt, and pepper. Cover the pan, and cook over low heat for 5 minutes or until most of the liquid is absorbed (the rice should still be moist). Stir in the chicken and raisins. Let the mixture cool.

Lay a sheet of filo horizontally on your work surface, and brush it lightly with melted butter. Lay a second sheet of filo over the first, and brush it with butter. Cut the filo in half crosswise. For each roll, place ½ cup filling in a band along one short edge of the filo, 3 inches from the edge; leave a 2-inch margin at either side. Fold the bottom edge over the filling. Fold in the sides. Roll up the filo jelly-roll style. Place the roll seam side down in an ungreased baking pan. Brush it with butter. Repeat this process with the remaining ingredients. If you are making the rolls ahead, cover and chill them up to 8 hours.

Preheat the oven to 350°F. Bake the rolls, uncovered, 20 to 25 minutes, or until they are golden brown.

Yield: 12 servings

Chimichangas

In Sonora, Mexico, chimichangas are wrapped in flour tortillas and deep-fried. I keep this filo-wrapped version in the freezer and bake them without thawing for an easy family meal.

½ pound lean ground pork
¼ pound ground chuck
½ medium onion, chopped
1 garlic clove, minced or pressed
1 *jalapeño* or *serrano* chile, seeded and minced
1 teaspoon brown sugar
1 teaspoon chili powder
¼ teaspoon salt
¼ teaspoon dried oregano
¼ teaspoon ground cumin
½ cup canned tomatoes, drained and finely chopped
1 tablespoon cider vinegar
2 tablespoons sliced pimiento-stuffed olives
9 sheets filo

5 tablespoons butter, melted, for brushing filo
Shredded lettuce, sour cream or guacamole, and salsa for condiments

Crumble the pork and beef into a wide frying pan. Stir them over medium-high heat until they are just browned. Add the onion, garlic, and chile. Reduce the heat to medium, and cook until the onion is tender. Drain off and discard the drippings. Add the brown sugar, chili powder, salt, oregano, cumin, tomatoes, vinegar, and olives. Simmer, stirring occasionally, for 15 minutes or until most of the liquid has evaporated. Let the mixture cool.

Lay a sheet of filo horizontally on your work surface, and brush it lightly with melted butter. Cover with a second sheet of filo. Brush it with butter. Cover with a third sheet of filo, and brush it with butter. Cut the filo in half crosswise. Spread about ½ cup filling in a band along one short edge of the filo, 2 inches from the edge; leave a 2-inch margin at either side. Fold the bottom edge over the filling. Fold in the sides. Roll up the filo jelly-roll style. Place the chimichanga seam side down in an ungreased baking pan, and brush it with butter. Repeat this process with the remaining ingredients. If you are making the chimichangas ahead, cover and chill them up to 24 hours.

Preheat the oven to 350°F. Bake the chimichangas, uncovered, 20 to 25 minutes, or until they are golden brown. Serve them hot.

Yield: 6 servings

Asparagus-Ham Rolls

This spring tonic goes together very quickly if you buy sandwich-size slices of ham and Swiss cheese.

8 large or 16 thin asparagus spears
2 (4-ounce) packages sandwich-size
   slices cooked ham
1 teaspoon Dijon mustard
4 (1-ounce) sandwich-size slices Swiss
   cheese
4 sheets filo
3 tablespoons butter, melted, for
   brushing filo

Creamy Mustard Sauce
3 tablespoons butter
3 tablespoons sour cream
1 tablespoon lemon juice
1 teaspoon Dijon mustard
Dash white pepper

Snap off and discard the tough asparagus ends. Place the asparagus in a wide frying pan with 1 inch of boiling water. Simmer 3 to 5 minutes, or until the asparagus is barely tender. Drain the asparagus, rinse it with cold water, and drain it again. Cut each spear in half.

For each roll, stack together two slices of ham. Coat the top slice with ¼ teaspoon mustard. Top with a slice of cheese and ¼ of the asparagus spears. Lay a sheet of filo horizontally on your work surface, and brush it lightly with melted butter. Lay a sheet of filo over the first, and brush it with butter. Cut the filo in half crosswise. Roll the ham around the filling and place the roll on the filo 2 inches from the bottom. Fold the bottom edge over the ham. Fold in the sides. Roll up the filo jelly-roll style. Place the roll seam side down in an ungreased baking pan. Brush it with butter. Repeat this process with the remaining ingredients. If you are making the rolls ahead, cover and chill them up to 8 hours.

Preheat the oven to 350°F. Bake the rolls, uncovered, for 20 minutes, or until they are golden brown.

While the rolls bake, make the sauce. Melt the butter in a small pan. Remove the pan from the heat and add the sour cream, lemon juice, mustard, and pepper. Whisk until smooth. Drizzle the sauce over the hot rolls.

Yield: 4 servings

Lamb Pilaf with Creamy Tahini Sauce

·ð·e·ð·e·ð·e·ð·e·ð·e·ð·e·ð·e·ð·e·ð·e·ð·e·ð·e·ð·e·ð·e·ð·e·ð·e·

I could make this blindfolded. During the years I was co-ower of a falafel shop we made this daily for our non-vegetarian clientele. We stuffed the pilaf into pocket bread, garnished it with lettuce and tomatoes, and topped it with our secret sauce. Divine, but messy to eat. Wrapped in filo, this is no longer street food. It's a stylish entree to serve with a platter of sliced tomatoes, lettuce, and cucumbers topped with more of the same secret sauce.

¼ cup pine nuts
2 tablespoons vegetable oil
1 medium onion, chopped
2 stalks celery, thinly sliced
1 garlic clove, minced or pressed
½ teaspoon each ground coriander and
   ground cumin
2 cups diced cooked lamb
3 cups cooked white long-grain rice
   (1 cup uncooked)
¼ cup chopped parsley

¼ cup beef or chicken broth
Salt and pepper to taste
12 sheets filo
½ cup butter, melted, for brushing filo

Creamy Tahini Sauce
½ cup cooked garbanzo beans
1 garlic clove
¾ cup water
½ cup tahini (sesame seed paste)
¼ cup lemon juice
¼ teaspoon each ground coriander and
   ground cumin
⅛ teaspoon salt
¼ cup chopped parsley

In a wide frying pan over low heat, cook the pine nuts in the oil until they are lightly browned. Lift them out with a slotted spoon, and set them aside.

Increase the heat to medium. Add the onion, celery, and garlic to the pan, and cook until the onion is soft. Stir in the coriander, cumin, and lamb, and cook for 2 minutes. Add the rice, parsley, and broth. Cover the pan, and cook over low heat for 5 minutes or until most of the liquid is absorbed (the rice should still be moist). Add the pine nuts, salt, and pepper. Let the pilaf cool.

Lay a sheet of filo horizontally on your work surface, and brush it lightly with melted butter. Lay another sheet over the first, and brush it with butter. Cut the filo in half crosswise. For each roll, place ½ cup filling in a band along one short edge of the filo, 3 inches from the edge; leave a 2-inch margin at either side. Fold the bottom edge over the filling. Fold in the sides. Roll the filo up jelly-roll style. Place the roll seam side down in an ungreased baking pan. Brush it with butter. Repeat this process with the remaining ingredients. If you are making the rolls ahead, cover and chill them up to 8 hours.

For the sauce, purée the garbanzos, the garlic, and ¼ cup of the water in a food processor or blender until smooth. Remove. In a food processor or in the large bowl of an electric mixer, blend the tahini and lemon juice until smooth. Add the remaining ½ cup water, coriander, cumin, and salt. Blend until smooth. Add the garbanzo purée, and blend until smooth. Transfer the sauce to a bowl, cover it, and chill the sauce. Just before serving, stir in the parsley. This sauce thickens on standing, so if necessary, stir in water to make it the consistency of softly whipped cream.

Preheat the oven to 350°F. Bake the rolls, uncovered, for 20 to 25 minutes, or until they are golden brown. Top each with a spoonful of sauce.

Yield: 12 servings

Pork in a Poke

One of the most convenient cuts of pork to buy is boneless pork loin chops. Tender and lean, they cook quickly—in the same time it takes the filo wrapper to brown.

2 tablespoons lemon juice
2 tablespoons olive oil
¼ teaspoon salt
¼ teaspoon dried rubbed sage
⅛ teaspoon ground black pepper
4 boneless center-cut pork loin chops,
    cut ¾ inch thick
4 sheets filo
2 tablespoons butter, melted, for
    brushing filo

In a 1-quart plastic bag, combine the lemon juice, 1 tablespoon of the oil, salt, sage, and pepper. Trim all fat from the meat. Place the meat in the bag, seal the bag, and chill for 2 hours. Lift meat from the marinade, and pat it dry with paper towels.

Heat the remaining 1 tablespoon oil in a wide frying pan over medium-high heat. Brown the chops for 3 minutes on each side. Let them cool.

Lay a sheet of filo horizontally on your work surface, and brush it lightly with melted butter. Lay a second sheet over the first, and brush it with butter. Cut the filo in half crosswise. For each packet, place a chop about 2 inches from a short end of the filo, centered between the long sides. Fold the short end of the filo over the meat. Fold in the long sides, then fold up the packet completely. Place the packet seam side down in an ungreased baking pan, and brush it with butter. Repeat this process with the remaining ingredients. If you are making the packets ahead, cover and chill them up to 8 hours.

Preheat the oven to 350°F. Bake the packets, uncovered, for 25 to 30 minutes, or until the filo is golden brown.

Yield: 4 servings

5
Desserts

Strudel

❧◆

If you grew up in a home where dessert was apple crisp or chocolate cake, you may think of strudel as something too difficult to be made by anyone other than an Old World cook. My first lesson in strudel making spanned half a day and almost convinced me this was true. With infinite patience, the dough was kneaded, rolled, and stretched into a 4-foot round, laid on a sheet, filled, and rolled into a plump cylinder large enough to feed the three generations of guests. Marvelous, but with filo so easy to use and the smaller rectangular sheets more manageable than a 4-foot round, I've never made strudel dough from scratch again. It's more fun to spend time on the fillings.

Whether you make a sweet strudel filled with fruit, cheese, or nuts, or a savory strudel, typically filled with cabbage or fish, the technique is the same. Place a clean towel on the work surface. (You'll use this later as a sling to help you roll the strudel.) Lay one sheet of filo on the towel and brush it lightly with melted butter (about 2 teaspoons). Top with a second sheet of filo and brush with butter. If the filling is not overly moist and you make a small strudel about 2 inches in diameter, two sheets will be enough. For a large strudel (3 to 4 inches in diameter) with a juicy filling, use four sheets of filo to absorb the moisture and to support the weight of the filling.

For juicy fillings, such as apple, sprinkle crumbs between the buttered filo layers to help absorb moisture. Crumbs also provide an interesting contrast in flavor and texture. Unseasoned dry bread crumbs, zwieback crumbs, graham cracker crumbs, cookie crumbs, and cake crumbs work well in sweet strudels; seasoned dry bread and cracker crumbs are good in savory strudels.

After stacking the sheets of filo, spoon the filling in a band about 2 inches from one edge. Fold the edge over the filling.

Using the towel to help you lift, roll the strudel jelly-roll style. Roll it compactly, but not too tightly, and don't fold in the sides. Most fillings need room to expand. (Strudel recipes with creamy fillings, found elsewhere in this book, will instruct you to fold in the sides.) Ease the strudel onto an ungreased baking pan and brush the top and sides with melted butter. To speed cleanup for strudels with juicy fillings, I line the pan with foil before baking.

How soon you must bake strudel after shaping it depends upon the filling. One made with uncooked fruit, such as apples, peaches, or apricots, should be baked at once. If it is left standing, the sugar in the filling liquifies and makes the filo soggy. As a rule of thumb, if the filling is dry enough so it will not soak into the filo, you can refrigerate the strudel for up to 8 hours before baking.

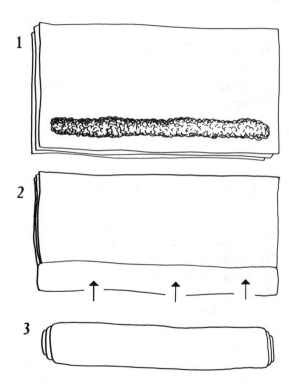

Apple Strudel

Don't be disappointed if this strudel doesn't last. It's not meant to! It tastes best within a few hours after baking. On the unlikely chance there are leftovers, re-crisp the filo by baking the strudel in a 200°F. oven a few minutes before serving.

2 tablespoons raisins
1 tablespoon brandy or rum
4 medium sweet-tart apples such as
   Granny Smith or Newtown Pippin
½ cup sugar
2 tablespoons finely chopped walnuts
½ teaspoon grated lemon zest
½ teaspoon lemon juice
¼ teaspoon ground cinnamon
Dash ground cloves
4 sheets filo
4 tablespoons butter, melted, for
   brushing filo
¼ cup zwieback crumbs or unseasoned
   dry bread crumbs

Powdered sugar
½ cup sour cream mixed with 2
   tablespoons half-and-half

Place the raisins and brandy in a small bowl; let them stand for 2 hours. Peel, core, and thinly slice the apples to make 4 cups. In a large bowl, combine the apples, raisins, brandy, sugar, walnuts, lemon zest, lemon juice, cinnamon, and cloves; mix well.

Preheat the oven to 375°F. Line a 12-by-18-inch baking pan with foil.

Place a towel horizontally on your work surface. Place one sheet of filo horizontally on the towel. Brush it lightly with melted butter; sprinkle it with 1 tablespoon of the crumbs. Repeat with the remaining filo, brushing each sheet lightly with butter and sprinkling with crumbs.

Spoon the apple filling and juices along one long side of the filo, 3 inches from the edge as illustrated on page 97. Fold the edge over the filling. Using the towel to help you lift, roll up the filo jelly-roll style; leave the ends open. Place the strudel in the prepared pan, seam side down. With a fork, prick the top in three or four places. Brush the top with butter.

Bake the strudel, uncovered, for 35 to 40 minutes, or until it is golden brown. If there is juice in the pan, bake the strudel 5 to 10 minutes more, until the juices evaporate. Let the strudel cool for about 45 minutes before cutting it; serve it warm. Dust each slice with powdered sugar. Pass the sour cream at the table.

Yield: 6 servings

Swiss Fruit Strudel

Sixteen servings may sound like oodles of strudel, but after you wrap this tangy-sweet dried fruit and nut filling in filo, you can freeze the unbaked rolls. It's a luscious pastry to have on hand for a special company meal or a quick family dessert.

2 (8-ounce) packages mixed dried fruit (pitted prunes, pears, apples, apricots, and peaches)
½ cup raisins
2 ¾ cups water
½ cup sugar
½ teaspoon ground cinnamon
¼ teaspoon ground cloves
2 tablespoons brandy
½ cup finely chopped walnuts
8 sheets filo
⅓ cup butter, melted, for brushing filo
Powdered sugar or sweetened whipped cream

In a 3-quart pan combine the mixed dried fruit, raisins, water, sugar, cinnamon, and cloves. Cook over medium heat until the sugar is dissolved. Cover the pan, and simmer over low heat, occasionally stirring and pushing the fruit down into the liquid, for 45 minutes, or until the fruit is tender and the liquid has been absorbed. Remove the pan from the heat, and stir briskly with a heavy wooden spoon to break up the fruit. The mixture should resemble a thick, coarse purée. Stir in the brandy and walnuts; let the mixture cool.

Place a towel vertically on your work surface. Lay a sheet of filo vertically on the towel, and brush it lightly with melted butter. Top with another sheet of filo, and brush it with butter. Spread 1 cup of filling in a band along one short edge of the filo, 2 inches from the edge; leave a 1-inch margin at either side. Fold the bottom edge over the filling. Fold in the sides. Using the towel to help you lift, roll up the filo jelly-roll style.

Place the strudel, seam side down, on an ungreased baking sheet. Brush it with butter. Repeat this process to make three more strudels.

Cover and chill the strudels if you plan to bake them within 24 hours. For longer storage, freeze them solid on the baking sheet, then transfer them to sealable plastic bags and return them to the freezer.

To bake the strudels, preheat the oven to 375°F. Bake the strudels, uncovered, for 20 minutes if chilled (25 to 30 minutes if frozen) or until they are golden brown. Let them cool for at least 30 minutes before cutting them. Serve them warm or at room temperature, dusted with powdered sugar or topped with whipped cream.

Yield: 16 servings (4 strudels)

Hungarian Almond Strudel

⅓ cup unblanched almonds
½ cup currant jelly
2 eggs, separated
3 tablespoons sugar
½ teaspoon each grated lemon zest
   and orange zest
6 sheets filo
4 tablespoons butter, melted, for
   brushing filo

Preheat the oven to 350°F. Toast the nuts for 10 minutes or until they are lightly browned. Let them cool, then very finely chop them.

Melt the jelly in a small pan over low heat, whisking it until smooth. In a bowl, whisk together the egg yolks and sugar until they are thick and creamy. Stir in the lemon and orange zests and almonds. In another bowl, beat egg whites until they hold stiff peaks. Fold into almond mixture.

Place one sheet of filo horizontally on your work surface. Brush the right half lightly with melted butter. Fold over the left half to cover the buttered side. Brush ½ teaspoon of the jelly along one short side of the filo, 2 inches from the bottom edge. Lightly brush butter over the rest of the folded sheet. Spoon ¼ cup of the egg-almond mixture over the jelly, 2 inches from the bottom; leave a 1-inch margin at either side. Fold the bottom edge over the filling. Fold in the sides. Fold up the filo loosely to make a packet about 6 inches by 2 inches. Place the packet seam side down in an ungreased baking pan; brush it with butter. Repeat to make five more strudels.

Bake the strudels at 350°F. for 20 minutes, or until they are puffed and golden brown. Let them cool for at least 15 minutes before serving. Serve them warm or at room temperature. Just before serving, reheat the jelly to melt it; drizzle a spoonful over each strudel.

Yield: 6 servings

Cherry-Almond Strudel

¼ cup blanched almonds
1 cup stemmed and pitted, fresh dark
    sweet cherries, or 1 cup frozen
    unsweetened pitted dark sweet
    cherries, thawed
¼ cup sugar
3 graham crackers, finely crushed
2 tablespoons butter, melted
½ teaspoon grated lemon zest
3 sheets filo
3 tablespoons butter, melted, for
    brushing filo
3 tablespoons powdered sugar mixed
    with 1 teaspoon lemon juice

Preheat the oven to 350°F. Toast the nuts for 8 to 10 minutes, or until they are lightly browned. Let them cool, then very finely chop them.

Increase the oven temperature to 375°F. In a bowl, combine the cherries, almonds, sugar, graham cracker crumbs, the 2 table-spoons melted butter, and lemon zest.

Place a towel vertically on your work surface. Stack the filo vertically on the towel, brushing each sheet lightly with melted butter as you stack. Spoon the cherry filling along one short side, 2 inches from the edge. Fold the edge over the filling. Using the towel to help you lift, roll up the filo jelly-roll style; leave the ends open. If one or two cherries or a few crumbs fall out of the ends, tuck them back inside the roll. Place the strudel in an ungreased baking pan, seam side down. Brush it with butter.

Bake the strudel 30 to 35 minutes, or until it is golden brown. Brush the powdered sugar–lemon mixture over the top. Let the strudel cool for at least 30 minutes before cutting it; serve it warm or at room temperature.

Yield: 4 servings

Baklava

Of all the Greek pastries made with filo, baklava is the most well known and widely enjoyed, and no one makes a more delectable version than this one, from Lou Pappas, free-lance food writer and cookbook author. Her almond-walnut filling is perfumed with lemon zest and cinnamon, and the baklava *steeps in a fragrant honey syrup after baking. To achieve a crispy, still-moist pastry, it is essential to pour cool syrup over hot pastry, or hot syrup over cool pastry—always have the temperature of the syrup and pastry at opposite extremes.*

Honey Syrup
¾ cup sugar
¾ cup water
1 3-inch cinnamon stick
1 ½ cups honey
1 pound (3 cups) almonds, finely
  chopped
1 pound (4 cups) walnuts, finely
  chopped

½ cup sugar
2 teaspoons grated lemon zest
2 teaspoons ground cinnamon
1 ½ cups (¾ pound) unsalted butter,
  melted, for brushing filo
1 pound filo

To make the syrup, combine the sugar, water, and cinnamon stick in a 2-quart pan. Bring to a boil, stirring occasionally until the sugar dissolves. Add the honey, and stir over low heat heat just until blended. Remove the pan from the heat. Let the syrup cool, then discard the cinnamon stick.

Preheat the oven to 300°F. Toast the nuts for 10 minutes, or until they are lightly browned; let them cool. Increase the oven temperature to 325°F.

Combine the sugar, lemon zest, and cinnamon in a large bowl. Mash them together with the back of a spoon to blend the citrus oil with the sugar. Add the toasted nuts;

mix lightly.

Butter a 9-by-13-inch baking pan. Line the pan with three sheets of filo, brushing each sheet lightly with melted butter and letting the filo overlap the sides of the pan. Sprinkle with about ½ cup of the nut mixture. Top with two sheets of buttered filo, letting the filo overlap the sides of the pan, and ½ cup more nuts. Repeat this process, alternating two sheets of buttered filo and the nut mixture, ending with the filo. Fold the overhanging filo over the filling. Fold one more sheet of filo to fit the pan; place it over the top, and brush with butter. Using a sharp knife, cut through only the top layer, making lengthwise strips 1 ½ inches wide. Then cut diagonally, making diamonds.

Bake the *baklava* for 1 hour, or until it is golden brown. Place the pan on a rack; cut through the diamonds completely with a sharp knife. Pour the cool honey syrup over the hot *baklava*. Let the baklava stand, uncovered, for at least 2 hours before serving. Store it covered, at room temperature up to 3 days; freeze it for longer storage.

Yield: 4 dozen pieces

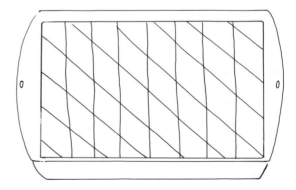

Bourma

You need a long ¼-inch wooden dowel to shape this pretty Armenian pastry that tastes similar to baklava. *The shaping technique is not diffi-cult, but you must work with filo that is very supple or the pastry will crack when it's crinkled on the dowel. Check the condition of your filo. If you have an opened package that has dry edges, choose another shape and wait until you open a fresh package to have fun with* bourma.

Syrup
1 cup sugar
1 cup water
2 teaspoons lemon juice
1 2-inch cinnamon stick
2 tablespoons honey

1 cup walnuts, finely chopped
4 pieces zwieback or 6 graham crackers, finely crushed
2 tablespoons sugar
½ teaspoon ground cinnamon

¾ cup unsalted butter, melted, for brushing filo
20 sheets filo

To make the syrup, combine the sugar, water, lemon juice, and cinnamon stick in a 2-quart pan. Bring to a boil, stirring occa-sionally until the sugar dissolves. Cook the syrup, without stirring, over medium-low heat until a candy thermometer registers 218° to 220°F. or syrup dropped from a metal spoon falls in a sheet, about 15 min-utes. Remove the pan from the heat and stir in the honey. Let the syrup cool, then dis-card the cinnamon stick.

Preheat the oven to 350°F. In a bowl, combine the walnuts, zwieback or graham cracker crumbs, 2 tablespoons sugar, and cinnamon. Place one sheet of filo horizon-tally on your work surface. Brush it lightly with melted butter. Spoon 2 tablespoons of the nut mixture in a band along one long edge, 2 inches from the edge; leave a 1-inch margin at either side. Fold in the sides. Fold the long edge over the filling. Place a 24-inch piece of ¼-inch wooden dowel on top of the filling. Loosely roll up the filo jelly-roll style. Gently push the roll along both ends of the dowel toward the center, crinkling it to about half its original length. Do not crinkle the filo too tightly. Pull out the dowel. Place the crinkled roll in an ungreased baking pan. Cut it into 2-inch lengths. Brush it with butter. Repeat this process with the remaining ingredients.

Bake the *bourma* for 20 minutes, or until the filo is crisp and golden brown. With your fingers or tongs, dip the hot pastries in the cool syrup. Drain them briefly, and place them on a platter. Let them stand, uncovered, for 2 hours before serving. Store them, covered, at room temperature up to 3 days; freeze them for longer storage.

Yield: About 40 pastries

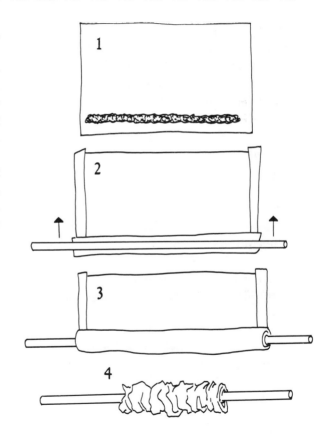

Nightingale's Nests

This Turkish version of individual baklavas *is coiled into a nest and topped with walnuts and pistachio nuts. Please don't be tempted to use more than 1 tablespoon filling for each pastry. If you add more, the rolled filo will be too rigid to roll into a nest.*

Syrup

2 cups sugar
1 cup water
1 2-inch strip lemon zest
1 tablespoon lemon juice
½ teaspoon rose water

1 cup walnuts, finely chopped
1 cup pistachio nuts, finely chopped
2 tablespoons sugar
20 sheets filo
¾ cup unsalted butter, melted, for brushing filo

To make the syrup, combine the sugar, water, lemon zest, and lemon juice in a 2-quart pan. Bring the mixture to a boil, stirring occasionally until the sugar dissolves. Cook, without stirring, over medium-low heat until a candy thermometer registers 218° to 220°F. or syrup dropped from a metal spoon falls in a sheet, about 10 minutes. Remove the pan from the heat; discard the lemon zest. Stir in the rose water, and let the syrup cool.

Preheat the oven to 350°F. In a bowl, combine the walnuts and pistachio nuts. Take out ⅔ cup nuts, and reserve them. Stir the sugar into the remaining nuts.

Spread one sheet of filo horizontally on your work surface. Brush the top half lightly with melted butter. Fold the bottom half over to cover the buttered half. Brush the filo lightly with butter. Spoon 1 tablespoon of the sugared nut mixture in a band 1 inch from the folded edge. Fold the edge over the filling. Roll up the filo to within 1 ½ inches of the other edge. Roll the roll loosely to make a 2 ½-to 3-inch circle. Press the free edges of filo into the center of the cylinder to form a bottom for the nest. Place the nest in an ungreased baking pan. Brush it with butter. Repeat this process with the remaining ingredients to make 20 nests.

Bake the pastries for 25 to 30 minutes or until they are golden. Pour the cooled syrup over the hot pastries. Let them stand 1 hour. Sprinkle the reserved nuts in the center of the pastries. Store them, covered, at room temperature up to 3 days; freeze them for longer storage.

Yield: 20 pastries

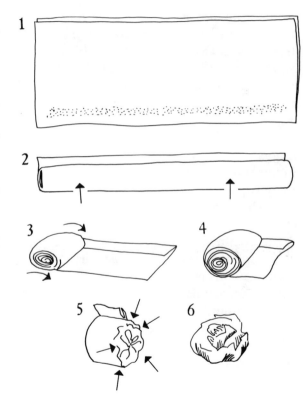

Galatoboriko

Of the many versions of this Greek custard pastry, the best I've eaten comes from my friend Marguerite Dalienes. The filling is rich and creamy, not overly sweet. Because it is showered with powdered sugar rather than soaked in heavy syrup, the filo wrapper remains light and crisp.

7 eggs
4 cups milk
1 cup sugar
½ cup butter
Dash salt
½ cup cream of rice cereal
1 tablespoon cornstarch mixed with 2
    tablespoons cold milk
1 teaspoon vanilla
About 2 pounds filo
1 ½ cups unsalted butter, melted, for
    brushing filo
Powdered sugar

In a medium bowl, beat the eggs well; set the bowl aside.

In a heavy 3-quart pan, scald the milk. Add the sugar, ½ cup butter, and salt; cook over medium heat until the butter melts. Gradually stir in the cereal. Stirring constantly, cook until the mixture comes to a full rolling boil. Remove the pan from the heat. Stir the eggs while adding a little of the hot cereal mixture to them. Return the egg mixture to the pan. Add the cornstarch-milk mixture. Place the pan over low heat. Stirring, cook just until the mixture bubbles gently. Remove it from the heat, and let it cool. Stir in the vanilla.

Lay a sheet of filo horizontally on your work surface, and brush it lightly with melted butter. Top with another sheet of filo, and brush it with butter. Cut the filo in half crosswise. For each pastry, spread 2 teaspoons of the filling in a band along one short edge of the filo, 1 inch from the edge;

leave a 2-inch margin at either side. Fold the bottom edge over the filling. Fold in the sides. Roll up the filo jelly-roll style to make a roll about 5 inches by 1 inch. Place the roll seam side down in an ungreased baking pan. Brush it with butter. Repeat this process with the remaining ingredients. Cover and chill the rolls if you plan to bake them within 24 hours. For longer storage, freeze them solid in baking pans, then transfer them to sealable plastic bags and return them to the freezer.

Preheat the oven to 375°F. Bake the pastries for 15 minutes (20 minutes if they are frozen) or until they are golden brown. Transfer them to a rack. Dust them heavily on both sides with powdered sugar. Serve them at room temperature.

Yield: About 80 pastries

Napoleons

I have to admit I've never made classic French Napoleans. I've ordered them from bakeries and chosen them from pastry trays in restaurants, but somehow I begrudge the time it takes to prepare the requisite puff pastry. Napoleans are fun to eat—the creamy filling goes squish, the crispy strips go crunch—so I make the pastries from stacks of filo.

If you finish a filo wrapping session and end up with a few extra sheets of dough, consider taking 5 minutes more to make pastries for Napoleons. You needn't complete the final assembly right away; the baked strips will keep for several days.

To make Napoleon pastries, stack five sheets of filo on your work surface, brushing each sheet lightly with melted regular or unsalted butter as you stack. Butter the top sheet. If the edges of the filo look dry, don't be tempted to brush them with extra butter; too much butter makes filo soggy rather than crisp.

Cut the stack in any size you wish from 3-inch squares to bite-size rectangles. Traditional Napoleons meaure about 2 by 3 inches. For a show-stopper dessert, cut large strips about 5 by 12 inches.

Preheat the oven to 350°F. Arrange the cut stacks, side by side, on an ungreased baking sheet. With a water mister, very lightly spray the top of the filo with water. Bake the pastries 8 to 10 minutes, or until they are golden brown. Place the pan on a rack, and let them cool. Store the pastries in an airtight container for up to 3 days. If the pastries lose their crispness, heat them in a 200°F. oven for 5 minutes a few hours before filling them.

Chocolate Napoleons

Use a very good chocolate to make this filling. A dark chocolate eating bar works well.

3 tablespoons milk
2 ounces semisweet chocolate (half of a 4-ounce bar), broken into pieces
¼ teaspoon vanilla
½ cup heavy cream
12 Napoleon pastries, each 2 by 3 inches (page 112)
Powdered sugar

Heat the milk to simmering in a 1-quart pan. Remove the pan from the heat, add the chocolate, and whisk until the chocolate is melted and the mixture is smooth. Stir in the vanilla. Chill the mixture until it is slightly thickened but not firm, about 30 minutes.

Beat the cream until soft peaks form. Add the chocolate, and beat until stiff. Use the filling at once, or cover and chill it up to 24 hours.

To assemble the Napoleons, spoon the chocolate cream onto six of the pastries; spread it level. Top each pastry with one of the remaining six pastries; sprinkle generously with powdered sugar. Serve the Napoleons immediately, or chill them, lightly covered, up to 1 hour.

Yield: 6 servings

Schroeder's Blueberry Squares

For more than three decades, Schroeder's Restaurant in San Francisco has delighted diners with ethereal desserts. This adaptation of their blueberry squares is wonderful with cherries, too.

1 (3-ounce) package cream cheese, softened
3 tablespoons powdered sugar
½ teaspoon vanilla
½ teaspoon grated lemon zest
½ cup heavy cream
1 cup fresh blueberries or pitted and halved sweet cherries
10 Napoleon pastries, each 3 inches square (page 112)
Powdered sugar

In a bowl, beat the cream cheese, 3 tablespoons powdered sugar, vanilla, and lemon zest until smooth.

In another bowl, beat the cream until stiff. Fold in the cream cheese until the mixture is evenly blended. Cover and chill it up to 8 hours. Just before serving, fold in the blueberries or cherries. Spoon the filling onto five of the pastries; spread it level. Top each pastry with one of the remaining five pastries; sprinkle generously with powdered sugar.

Yield: 5 servings

Strawberry Napoleon

You can prepare the sabayon sauce up to 4 hours ahead, but assemble the Napoleon just before serving so that the pastry does not become soggy. For ease of cutting, use a serrated knife.

2 egg yolks
3 tablespoons sugar
⅓ cup champagne or white wine
¼ cup heavy cream
2 cups strawberries, hulled and sliced
2 tablespoons sugar
3 Napoleon pastries, each 5 by 12 inches (page 112)
Powdered sugar

In the top of a double boiler, whisk together the egg yolks and 3 tablespoons sugar until thick and pale yellow. Add the champagne or wine. Pour hot water into the bottom of the double boiler, making sure the water won't touch the bottom of the top pan. Heat the water just to simmering, then set the top pan in place. Whisk the sauce mixture vigorously and constantly for 8 minutes, or until the sauce is thick and foamy. Don't let the sauce come to a boil, or it will curdle. Pour the sabayon sauce into a bowl, and refrigerate it until cold.

One hour before serving, combine the strawberries and 2 tablespoons sugar in a bowl; let them stand at room temperature.

Just before serving, beat the cream until stiff. Fold it into the sabayon sauce.

To assemble the Napoleon, place one pastry on a platter. Cover with half the sabayon cream and half the strawberries. Top with another pastry, and cover with the remaining sabayon cream and strawberries. Place the third pastry on top; dust generously with powdered sugar. Serve at once.

Yield: 6 servings

Raspberry-Lemon Napoleon

For a classic Napoleon, Chef Abby Nash makes puff pastry with ease, but he is quick to point out that "filo stands in nicely for the puff pastry strips and is so much easier!" I use five layers of filo for the strips; he uses eight layers of filo in his tart-sweet Napoleon. Which proves that in cooking there is more than one way to reach a very delicious conclusion.

Lemon Curd
4 egg yolks
¼ cup sugar
Grated zest and juice of 1 ½ lemons
1 tablespoon milk
4 tablespoons unsalted butter, cut into 4 pieces

Raspberry Sauce
1 ½ cups raspberries
2 tablespoons sugar
1 teaspoon lemon juice

½ cup heavy cream
3 Napoleon pastries, each 12 by 3 inches (page 112; use 8 layers of filo instead of 5, if desired)
1 ½ cups whole raspberries
Powdered sugar

For the filling, in a small heavy saucepan, combine the egg yolks and sugar; whisk until well mixed. Whisk in the lemon zest, lemon juice, and milk. Add the butter. Whisking constantly, cook the mixture over medium-low heat until it is smooth and thickened; do not allow it to boil. Remove the lemon curd from the heat; let it stand until cool, whisking occasionally. Cover and chill it up to 2 days.

For the sauce, purée the raspberries, sugar, and lemon juice in a blender or food processor. Strain the puree to remove the seeds. Cover and chill it

One hour before serving, beat the cream

until it holds soft peaks. Fold it into the chilled lemon curd.

To assemble the Napoleon, place one pastry on a platter. Cover with half the lemon curd, half the raspberry sauce, and half the whole raspberries. Top with another pastry, and cover with the remaining lemon curd, raspberry sauce, and whole raspberries. Place the third pastry on top; dust generously with powdered sugar.

Yield: 6 servings

Deep-Dish Gingered Peach Pie

Making filo-topped pie is child's play. Pour the filling into a baking dish, cover with a stack of buttered filo rounds, and bake. If you're in a hurry, use the filo directly from the refrigerator. Since the crust doesn't require fancy folding, it's not essential to let the filo warm to room temperature.

4 cups sliced peeled peaches or sliced unpeeled nectarines
½ cup sugar
1 tablespoon finely chopped crystallized ginger
1 ½ tablespoons cornstarch
2 teaspoons lemon juice
4 or 8 sheets filo
4 to 6 tablespoons butter, melted, for brushing filo

Preheat the oven to 375° F. In a large bowl, combine the peaches, sugar, ginger, cornstarch, and lemon juice; mix well. Turn the mixture into a 1-quart soufflé dish or a baking dish at least 2 inches deep. Measure the diameter of your baking dish. For a dish with a 6-inch diameter, cut four sheets of filo in half crosswise to make rectangles about 8 by 12 inches. Stack the half sheets, brushing each sheet lightly with melted butter as you stack. Using the tip of a sharp knife and an 8-inch plate as a guide, cut out a circle. (For a larger baking dish, use 8 sheets of filo; cut round 2 inches larger than the diameter of the dish.) Place the filo over the peaches. Roll the edges down toward the center so the crust fits snugly in the dish. Cut a slit in the top, and brush with butter.

Bake the pie for 40 minutes, or until the peaches are juicy and the filo is golden brown. Let the pie stand for about 30 minutes before serving.

Yield: 4 servings

Shells

When you work with filo, you don't need to be a whiz with a rolling pin to make shells for individual tarts or tartlets. (Large tart shells work best made with a sturdy sweet butter pastry that won't crumble when cut.) Filo shells are not only quick and easy, they can be formed into unusual fanciful shapes. As a bonus, filo gives you crisp shells with fewer calories than classic pastry.

For tart pans you can use heat-proof glass custard cups, metal muffin cups, foil tart pans, or fluted metal tartlet pans. Smooth muffin cups and custard cups are easiest to use. Filo tends to stick in pans with ridges, so if you use them, butter the pans well. Metal pans brown the filo more rapidly than glass. Check the browning of the shells as they bake.

When cutting circles, use a plate, a bowl, or a circle of heavy cardboard as a template. Cut the filo with the tip of a sharp knife.

Although my recipes call for butter, you may want to experiment with some of the nut oils. Walnut oil and almond oil are delicious. Hazelnut oil is more potent and is best diluted with melted butter.

Bake all of the following tart shells in a preheated 350°F. oven for 10 to 15 minutes or until they are golden brown. Remove from the oven and cool on racks. Store in an airtight container at room temperature for up to 3 days. For longer storage, pack in rigid containers and freeze. If the shells lose their crispness, reheat in a 200°F. oven for 5 minutes a few hours before filling.

Tart Shells
Stack four sheets of filo, brushing each sheet lightly with melted butter (about 2 teaspoons) as you stack. For large shells, cut 6-inch circles; place them in buttered 4 ½-inch custard cups. For small shells, cut 5-inch circles; place them in buttered 3 ½-inch custard cups.

Tartlet Shells

Follow the directions for tart shells but use only 3 sheets of filo. Cut out 2 ½-inch circles. Place them in buttered 1 ½-inch muffin cups.

Tulip Shells

Stack four sheets of filo, brushing each sheet lightly with melted butter (about 2 teaspoons) as you stack. Cut the stack into six 6-inch squares. Place each square in a buttered 2 ½-inch muffin cup.

Ruffled Shells

Stack four sheets of filo, brushing each sheet lightly with melted butter (about 2 teaspoons) as you stack. Cut the stack into 12 4-inch squares. Set one square atop another square at a 45° angle so there are eight corners. Place the filo in a buttered 2 ½-inch muffin cup. Repeat the process with the remaining squares to make six ruffled shells.

Free-Form Shells

Cut two sheets of filo to make two 12-inch squares. Brush one square lightly with melted butter (about 2 teaspoons); top with the second square, and brush with butter. Gently press the center of the square into a buttered 4 ½-inch custard cup. Press in the filo to line the cup. Roll and fold the overhanging edges so they resemble crumpled tissue paper. Brush the edges lightly with butter.

Plum Pastries

A light and lovely dessert that's perfect for calorie counters. Use a combination of plum varieties if you wish, but include some with purple skins to give the poached fruit a ruby-red color.

1 pound plums, pitted and quartered
¼ cup sugar
¼ cup water
1 2-inch cinnamon stick
⅓ cup sour cream or yogurt
4 small tart shells (page 119)

In a medium pan, combine the plums, sugar, water, and cinnamon stick. Bring to a boil, stirring, over medium heat. Reduce the heat, cover the pan, and simmer 6 to 8 minutes, or until the plums are tender when pierced. Remove the pan from the heat; discard the cinnamon stick. Let the plums cool; cover and chill them up to 2 days.

To assemble the pastries, whisk together the sour cream and 1 tablespoon of the plum syrup in a small bowl. Lift the plums from the remaining syrup with a slotted spoon, and divide them among the filo shells. Drizzle the sour cream sauce over each pastry. Serve at once.

Yield: 4 servings

Strawberry Tarts with Yogurt Sauce

This tangy, light sauce tastes good over any combination of fresh fruit or berries.

1 cup plain yogurt
2 tablespoons frozen orange juice
    concentrate, thawed
1 ½ tablespoons honey
½ teaspoon grated lemon zest
¼ teaspoon ground nutmeg
2 cups hulled and sliced strawberries
2 kiwi fruit, peeled and diced
6 free-form shells (page 120)

In a bowl combine the yogurt, orange juice concentrate, honey, lemon zest, and nutmeg; whisk until smooth. Cover the sauce, and chill it 2 hours for the flavors to blend, or as long as 2 days. To assemble the tarts, divide the strawberries and kiwi fruit among the filo shells. Pour the yogurt sauce over the fruit. Serve at once.

Yield: 6 servings.

White Chocolate Cups with Raspberry Sauce

Elegant-looking yet a breeze to prepare, this chocolate lover's delight can be doubled or tripled for a large event.

1 bar (4 ounces) white chocolate,
   broken into pieces
2 egg whites
2 tablespoons sugar
1 cup heavy cream
½ teaspoon vanilla
1 package (12 ounces) frozen
   raspberries in light syrup, thawed
5 tulip shells or ruffled shells
   (page 120)

In the top of a double boiler, melt the chocolate over barely simmering water. Remove the top pan, and set it aside.

In a small bowl, beat the egg whites until foamy. Gradually mix in the sugar, beating until stiff. With a whisk, fold in the hot melted chocolate. The mixture will look slightly curdled at first but, with folding, it will become smooth.

In another bowl, beat the cream until stiff. Stir in the vanilla, then fold in the chocolate mixture. You can cover and chill it up to 8 hours.

In a blender or food processor, purée the raspberries and syrup. Strain the purée to remove the seeds.

To assemble the cups, spoon about ⅓ cup white chocolate cream into each filo shell. Drizzle the raspberry sauce over the tops. Serve at once.

Yield: 5 servings

Cannoli

Sicilian cooks make cannoli shells by wrapping pastry strips around metal molds and frying them in deep fat. For a lighter, easier version, serve this creamy dessert in crisp filo shells.

1 cup ricotta cheese
2 tablespoons powdered sugar
¼ teaspoon vanilla
2 tablespoons finely chopped
   bittersweet chocolate
2 tablespoons orange marmalade
2 tablespoons Cointreau or other
   orange-flavored liqueur
½ cup heavy cream
6 tulip shells or ruffled shells
   (page 120)
Chocolate curls for garnish

In a bowl, combine the ricotta cheese, sugar, and vanilla; whisk until smooth. Stir in the chocolate, marmalade, and Cointreau.

In another bowl, beat the cream until stiff. Fold in the ricotta mixture. If you are making the filling ahead, cover and chill it up to 8 hours.

Just before serving, spoon about ⅓ cup filling into each shell. Garnish with chocolate curls.

Yield: 6 servings

Mango Cream Cups

If you are looking for a dessert to complement a Mexican or Southwestern menu, try this combination of mango and orange. Use fresh mangoes when they are in season or look for canned mangoes at a Mexican market.

1 (15-ounce) can mangoes, drained
1 tablespoon lime juice
2 tablespoons sugar
2 oranges
½ cup heavy cream
¼ cup chopped pecans
6 small tart shells (page 119)
Mint sprigs for garnish

In a food processor or blender, blend the mangoes to make 1 cup purée. Stir in the lime juice and sugar.

Remove the peel and white membrane from the oranges; lift out the segments. Cut each segment in half, and place the pieces in a sieve to drain. Cover the mango purée and orange segments, and chill them up to 24 hours.

In a bowl, beat the cream until stiff. Fold in the mango purée, orange segments, and pecans. Spoon the filling into filo shells, and garnish each shell with a sprig of mint. Serve at once.

Yield: 6 servings

Butterscotch-Almond Sundaes

If you want to gild the lily—your favorite ice cream—go all the way with a crisp filo case, rich buttery sauce, and toasted nuts. Yum.

¼ cup sliced almonds
½ cup packed brown sugar
⅓ cup heavy cream
3 tablespoons butter
1 pint vanilla ice cream
4 large tart shells (page 119)

Preheat the oven to 300°F. Toast the nuts for 10 minutes, or until they are lightly browned.

Combine the brown sugar, cream, and butter in a 2-quart pan. Cook over medium heat, stirring occasionally, until the sugar is dissolved. Reduce the heat to low and simmer 2 minutes. Let the sauce cool; it will thicken slightly. If you are making it ahead, pour it into a jar, cover it, and chill it up to 3 days. To reheat the sauce, place the jar in a small pan of simmering water.

To serve the sundaes, place a scoop of ice cream in each filo shell, top with the butterscotch sauce, and sprinkle with almonds.

Yield: 4 servings

Fruit and Berry Tarts

Tea time, or any time, jewel-like fruit tarts are always welcome. You can make the components ahead of time, but assemble the tarts only 2 hours before serving.

Pastry Cream
2 eggs
2 egg yolks
½ cup sugar
¼ cup all-purpose flour
1 ½ cups milk
½ teaspoon vanilla
2 tablespoons butter

**10 small tart shells or 30 tartlet shells
(page 119, 120)**
Fruit and berries of your choice

In a medium bowl, beat the eggs and egg yolks well. Add the sugar and flour, and whisk until smooth.

In a 2-quart pan over medium heat, scald the milk. Whisking constantly, pour half the milk into the egg mixture. Pour the egg mixture back into the pan; whisk to combine. Cook the mixture, stirring constantly, over medium-low heat until it comes to a boil and thickens, 2 to 3 minutes. Continue to stir and simmer for 1 minute. Remove the pan from the heat, and stir in the vanilla and butter. Pour the pastry cream through a sieve into a bowl. Cover the surface of the pastry cream with plastic wrap. When the pastry cream is cool, chill it. You can store it in the refrigerator up to 3 days.

To assemble the tarts, place about 3 tablespoons pastry cream in each tart shell or 1 tablespoon in each tartlet shell. Cover the entire surface of the pastry cream with berries or sliced fruit. Serve the tarts immediately, or chill them up to 2 hours.

Yield: 10 tarts or 30 tartlets

Chinese Crackers

It's hard to imagine a Chinese meal ending without a fortune cookie, but these twists, which look like the party favor "crackers," make a tastier sweet conclusion.

¼ cup sesame seeds
½ cup finely chopped pitted dates
½ cup sweetened flaked coconut
¼ cup sugar
2 tablespoons orange juice
6 sheets filo
4 tablespoons butter, melted, for
   brushing filo

Toast the sesame seeds in an ungreased frying pan over medium heat, shaking the pan often, until the seeds are golden, about 2 minutes. Place them in a bowl, and let them cool briefly. Add the dates, coconut, and sugar. Crumble the mixture with your fingers until the ingredients are well combined. Stir in the orange juice.

Preheat the oven to 350°F. Brush one sheet of filo lightly with melted butter. Cut the filo in half lengthwise and crosswise to make four equal pieces. Place 2 teaspoons filling along a long edge of one piece. Roll the filo into a cylinder; crimp filo 1 inch from the ends to look like a party favor. Place the cylinder in an ungreased baking pan, and brush it with butter. Repeat this process with the remaining ingredients.

Bake the crackers, uncovered, for 15 minutes, or until the ends of the filo are golden brown. Transfer them to a rack, and let them cool. Store them in an airtight container.

Yield: 2 dozen pastries

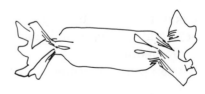

Apricot Turnovers

These turnovers are perfect when you are packing lunches or any time you want a sweet that can be eaten out of hand.

1 cup dried apricots
¾ cup water
¾ cup sugar
1 tablespoon lemon juice
¼ cup finely chopped almonds
12 sheets filo
½ cup butter, melted, for brushing filo

In a 2-quart pan, simmer the apricots and water, covered, for 10 minutes. Add the sugar and lemon juice; simmer for 10 more minutes, or until the apricots are tender. Uncover the pan, and cook until most of the liquid has evaporated. In a food processor, purée the mixture to make a thick paste. Let it cool; stir in the almonds.

Preheat the oven to 350°F. Lay a sheet of filo horizontally on your work surface, and brush it lightly with melted butter. Top it with a second sheet of filo, and brush it with butter. Cut the filo crosswise into five equal strips. Place 2 teaspoons of the filling at the bottom of each strip. Fold the strips into triangles, as explained on page 13. Place the triangles seam side down in an ungreased baking pan. Brush them lightly with butter. Repeat this process with the remaining ingredients.

Bake the turnovers, uncovered, for 20 minutes, or until they are golden brown. Transfer them to a rack, and let them cool. Serve them at room temperature.

Yield: 30 turnovers

Apple Turnovers with Rum Sauce

Served warm with rum sauce, these are a festive dessert for parties. If you want to take them to a picnic, let the pastries cool, then shower them with powdered sugar.

To remove the apple cores easily, use a melon ball cutter.

1 cup sugar
1 cup water
6 tablespoons butter
3 large (1 ½ pounds) Granny Smith or Golden Delicious apples, halved lengthwise, cored, and peeled
6 sheets filo
4 tablespoons butter, melted, for brushing filo
2 tablespoons dark rum

In a 2-quart pan, combine the sugar, water, and 6 tablespoons butter. Cook over medium heat, stirring occasionally, until the sugar is dissolved. Add the apples to the pan, cover the pan, and simmer 8 to 10 minutes, or until the apples are tender but still hold their shape. With a slotted spoon, transfer the apples to a rack, and let them cool. Strain the syrup, and reserve it.

Place one sheet of filo horizontally on your work surface. Lightly brush the right half with melted butter. Fold over the left half to cover the buttered side. Brush the folded filo with butter. Place one apple half 3 inches from one short edge of filo, centered between the long sides. Fold the bottom edge over the apple; fold in the sides. Fold the filo completely, as illustrated on page 53, to make a packet about 3 inches by 4 inches. Place the packet seam side down in an ungreased baking pan. Brush it with butter. Repeat this process until all the apples are wrapped. If you are assembling the turnovers ahead, cover and chill them up to 8 hours.

Preheat the oven to 350°F. Bake the

turnovers, uncovered, for 20 to 25 minutes, or until the edges of the filo are golden brown. Let the turnovers cool for 15 minutes before serving. Meanwhile, cook the reserved syrup, uncovered, over medium heat until it thickens. Stir in the rum. Spoon the sauce over each turnover just before serving.

Yield: 6 servings

Pear Pouches

ੴ◆ਫ਼

If you've ever wrapped a bottle in tissue paper, you know how easy it is to stand the bottle in the center of the paper, gather the paper around the bottle and tie a ribbon around the bottle's neck, letting the ends of the paper extend prettily beyond the ribbon. This is the same technique you use to make pouches with one exception: the gathered filo below the ruffly top stays in place so you don't need to tie it with ribbon. (If you wrap a savory filling in a pouch, however, you could tie it with kampyo *page 78.)*

To keep the bottom of the pouch from becoming soggy, drain the pears well. If you wrap a very moist filling, protect the base by adding two 4- or 5-inch filo squares inside the bottom. I've made pouches with three and four half sheets of filo, but, for my taste, that creates too many mouthfuls of ruffles.

1 quart cold water
2 tablespoons lemon juice
4 small Bartlett or Bosc pears

1 cup dry red wine
½ cup sugar
1 2-inch strip lemon zest
1 2-inch cinnamon stick
2 tablespoons currant jelly
1 tablespoon cornstarch mixed with 2 tablespoons water
4 sheets filo
3 tablespoons butter, melted, for brushing filo
1 teaspoon sugar

Place water and lemon juice in a large bowl. Peel, quarter, and core the pears; cut each quarter in half. Drop the pears into the lemon-water to prevent discoloration.

In a 2-quart pan, combine the wine, ½ cup sugar, lemon zest, and cinnamon stick. Cook over medium heat, stirring occasionally, until the sugar is dissolved. Drain the pears, and place them in the pan. Cover the pan and simmer the pears 10 minutes, or until they are tender but still hold their shape. With a slotted spoon, transfer the pears to a colander, and let them cool.

Strain the syrup. Cook it, uncovered, over medium heat for 10 minutes, or until it is reduced to ½ cup. Stir in the currant jelly. When the jelly melts, add the cornstarch-water mixture and cook, stirring, for 30 seconds, or until the sauce thickens slightly. Let it cool.

For each pouch, cut one sheet of filo in half crosswise to make rectangles about 8 by 12 inches. Brush one half sheet with about 1 teaspoon melted butter. Place the other half sheet on top at right angles to the first. Brush the top with butter. Place a quarter of the drained pears in the center of the filo. Lift the ends of the filo up and around the filling, gathering them at the top. Press the filo together just above the filling to secure the pouch. Brush the ruffles lightly with butter; sprinkle them with ¼

teaspoon sugar. Place the pouch in a greased baking pan. Repeat this process until all the pouches are filled. If you are making them ahead, cover and chill them up to 2 hours.

Preheat the oven to 375°F. Bake the pouches, uncovered, for 12 to 15 minutes, or until the filo ruffles are lightly browned. Place each packet on a dessert plate, and spoon the sauce around the packet. Serve at once.

Yield: 4 servings

133

Index